Physical Science Grade 5
Table of Contents

Physical Science Grade 5
Introduction

We wake up in a new world every day. Our lives are caught in a whirlwind of change. New wonders are discovered almost daily. Technology is carrying us headlong into the 21st century. How will our children keep pace? We must provide them with the tools necessary to go forth into the future. Those tools can be found in a sound science education. One guidepost to a good foundation in science is the National Science Education Standards. This book adheres to these standards.

Young children are interested by almost everything around them. They constantly ask questions about how and why things work. They should be encouraged to observe their world, the things in it, and how things interact. They should take note of the properties of the Earth and its materials, distinguish one material from another, and then try to develop their own explanation of why things are the way they are. A basic understanding of science boosts students' understanding of the world around them.

As children learn more about their world, they should be encouraged to ask questions about how things in their world work, such as how a switch turns on power, what makes a carousel turn, and what causes an ice cube to melt.

Organization
Physical Science serves as a handy companion to the regular science curriculum. It is broken into three units: A Charge for Life, Keep on Moving!, and It Matters! Each unit contains concise background information on the unit's topics, as well as exercises and activities to reinforce students' knowledge and understanding of basic principles of science and the world around them.

- A Charge for Life: Students learn that electricity is a form of energy that makes other objects move. They will discover how static electricity is produced when electrons jump from one object to another and that lightning is an example of static electricity. Students will also explore different kinds of circuits and the reasons for fuses and breakers. Finally, students learn about magnets and how a magnetic field is used in modern technology.

- Keep on Moving!: Students begin to understand the basic concepts of motion, speed, velocity, and inertia. They experiment with Sir Isaac Newton's laws of motion and examine the need for seatbelts according to these principles.

- It Matters!: The unit briefly reviews the basic characteristics of the three states of matter and the proper scientific units of measurement. However, the majority of the unit focuses on physical and chemical changes, with particular emphasis on compounds, including acid and base substances.

This book contains three types of pages:
- Concise background information is provided for each unit. These pages are intended for the teacher's use or for helpers to read to the class.
- Exercises are included for use as tests or practice for the students. These pages are meant to be reproduced.
- Activity pages list the materials and steps necessary for students to complete a project. Questions for students to answer are also included on these pages as a type of performance assessment. As much as possible, these activities include most of the multiple intelligences so students can use their strengths to achieve a well-balanced learning style. These pages are also meant for reproduction for use by students.

Use

Physical Science is designed for independent use by students who have been introduced to the skills and concepts described. This book is meant to supplement the regular science curriculum; it is not meant to replace it. Copies of the activities can be given to individuals, pairs of students, or small groups for completion. They may also be used as a center activity. If students are familiar with the content, the worksheets may also be used as homework.

To begin, determine the implementation that fits your students' needs and your classroom structure. The following plan suggests a format for this implementation.

1. Explain the purpose of the worksheets to your students. Let them know that these activities will be fun as well as helpful.
2. Review the mechanics of how you want the students to work with the activities. Do you want them to work in groups? Are the activities for homework?
3. Decide how you would like to use the assessments. They can be given before and after a unit to determine progress, or only after a unit to assess how well the concepts have been learned. Determine whether you will send the tests home or keep them in students' portfolios.
4. Introduce students to the process and the purpose of the activities. Go over the directions. Work with children when they have difficulty. Work only a few pages at a time to avoid pressure.
5. Do a practice activity together.

The Scientific Method

Students can be more productive if they have a simple procedure to use in their science work. The scientific method is such a procedure. It is detailed here, and a reproducible page for students is included on page 7.

1. PROBLEM: Identify a problem or question to investigate.
2. HYPOTHESIS: Tell what you think will be the result of your investigation or activity.
3. EXPERIMENTATION: Perform the investigation or activity.
4. OBSERVATION: Make observations, and take notes about what you observe.
5. CONCLUSION: Draw conclusions from what you have observed.
6. COMPARISON: Does your conclusion agree with your hypothesis? If so, you have shown that your hypothesis was correct. If not, you need to change your hypothesis.
7. PRESENTATION: Prepare a presentation or report to share your findings.
8. RESOURCES: Include a list of resources used. Students need to give credit to people or books they used to help them with their work.

Hands-On Experience

An understanding of science is best promoted by hands-on experience. *Physical Science* provides a wide variety of activities for students to do. But students also need real-life exposure to their world. Playgrounds, parks, and vacant lots are handy study sites to observe many of nature's forces.

It is essential that students be given sufficient concrete examples of scientific concepts. Appropriate manipulatives can be bought or made from common everyday objects. Most of the activity pages can be completed with materials easily accessible to the students. Manipulatives that can be used to reinforce scientific skills are recommended on several of the activity pages.

Science Fair

Knowledge without application is wasted effort. Students should be encouraged to participate in their school science fair. To help facilitate this, each unit in *Physical Science* ends with a page of science fair ideas and projects. Also, on page 8 is a chart that will help students to organize their science fair work.

To help students develop a viable project, you might consider these guidelines:

- Decide whether to do individual or group projects.
- Help students choose a topic that interests them and that is manageable. Make sure a project is appropriate for a student's grade level and ability. Otherwise, that student might become frustrated. This does not mean that you should discourage a student's scientific curiosity. However, some projects are just not appropriate. Be sure, too, that you are familiar with the school's science fair guidelines. Some schools, for example, do not allow glass or any electrical or flammable projects. An exhibit also is usually restricted to three or four feet of table space.
- Encourage students to develop questions and to talk about their questions in class.
- Help students to decide on one question or problem.
- Help students to design a logical process for developing the project. Stress that the acquisition of materials is an important part of the project. Some projects also require strict schedules, so students must be willing and able to carry through with the process.

- Remind students that the scientific method will help them to organize their thoughts and activities. Students should keep track of their resources used, whether they are people or print materials. Encourage students to use the Internet to do research on their project.

Additional Notes

- Parent Communication: Send the Letter to Parents home with students so that parents will know what to expect and how they can best help their child.
- Bulletin Board: Display completed work to show student progress.
- Portfolios: You may want your students to maintain a portfolio of their completed exercises and activities, or of newspaper articles about current events in science. This portfolio can help you in performance assessment.
- Assessments: There are Assessments for each unit at the beginning of the book. You can use the tests as diagnostic tools by administering them before children begin the activities. After children have completed each unit, let them retake the unit test to see the progress they have made.
- Center Activities: Use the worksheets as a center activity to give students the opportunity to work cooperatively.
- Have fun: Working with these activities can be fun as well as meaningful for you and your students.

Physical Science Grade 5
Curriculum Correlation

Language Arts	131, 140
Math	26, 27, 28, 29, 31, 41, 47, 49, 50, 63, 64, 65, 66, 69, 70, 73, 74, 79, 80, 83, 89, 92, 104, 105, 109, 106, 110, 111, 112, 113, 114, 115, 116, 120, 123, 129, 130, 132, 137
Social Studies	23, 44, 45, 46, 49, 51, 60, 62, 68, 72, 75, 76, 77, 78, 86, 87, 89, 90, 118, 124, 138
Health/PE	52, 53, 54, 81, 82, 95, 97, 103, 123, 137, 138
Music/Art	33, 34, 36, 39, 42, 85, 126, 127, 128, 133, 135, 136, 138

FOSS Curriculum Correlation

The Full Option Science System™ (FOSS) was developed at the University of California at Berkeley. It is a coordinated science curriculum organized into four categories: Life Science; Physical Science; Earth Science; and Scientific Reasoning and Technology. Under each category are various modules that span two grade levels. The modules for this grade level are highlighted in the chart below.

Levers and Pulleys	See *Physical Science*, Grade 4.
Mixtures and Solutions	99-102, 117, 118, 120, 122, 123, 125, 126, 127-128, 129-130, 131, 132, 133, 136, 137, 138, 139, 140

Dear Parent,

During this school year, our class will be using an activity book to reinforce the science skills we are learning. By working together, we can be sure that your child not only masters these science skills but also becomes confident in his or her abilities.

From time to time, I may send home activity sheets. To help your child, please consider the following suggestions:

- Provide a quiet place to work.
- Go over the directions together.
- Help your child to obtain any materials that might be needed.
- Encourage your child to do his or her best.
- Check the activity when it is complete.
- Discuss the basic science ideas associated with the activity.

Help your child to maintain a positive attitude about the activities. Let your child know that each lesson provides an opportunity to have fun and to learn more about the world around us. Above all, enjoy this time you spend with your child. As your child's science skills develop, he or she will appreciate your support.

Thank you for your help.

Cordially,

Name _____ Date _____

The Scientific Method

Did you know you think and act like a scientist? You can prove it by following these steps when you have a problem. These steps are called the scientific method.

1. Problem: Identify a problem or question to investigate.

_____

_____

_____

2. Hypothesis: Tell what you think will be the result of your investigation or activity.

_____

_____

_____

3. Experimentation: Perform the investigation or activity.

_____

_____

4. Observation: Make observations, and take notes about what you observe.

_____

_____

_____

5. Conclusion: Draw conclusions from what you have observed.

_____

_____

_____

6. Comparison: Does your conclusion agree with your hypothesis? If so, you have shown that your hypothesis was correct. If not, you need to change your hypothesis.

_____

7. Presentation: Prepare a presentation or report to share your findings.

_____

8. Resources: Include a list of resources used. You need to give credit to people or books you used to help you with your work.

_____

_____

_____

Physical Science 5, SV 3764-X

The Science Fair

The science fair at your school is a good place to show your science skills and knowledge. Science fair projects can be several different types. You can do a demonstration, make a model, present a collection, or perform an experiment. You need to think about your project carefully so that it will show your best work. Use the scientific method to help you to organize your project. Here are some other things to consider:

Project Title _____

Working Plan	Date Due	Date Completed	Teacher Initials
1. Select topic			
2. Explore resources			
3. Start notebook			
4. Form hypothesis			
5. Find materials			
6. Investigate			
7. Prepare results			
8. Prepare summary			
9. Plan your display			
10. Construct your display			
11. Complete notebook			
12. Prepare for judging			

Write a brief paragraph describing the hypothesis, materials, and procedures you will include in your exhibit.

Be sure to plan your project carefully. Get all the materials and resources you need beforehand. Also, a good presentation should have plenty of visual aids, so use pictures, graphs, charts, and other things to make your project easier to understand.

Be sure to follow all the rules for your school science fair. Also, be prepared for the judging part. The judges will look for a neat, creative, well-organized display. They will want to see a clear and thorough presentation of your data and resources. Finally, they will want to see that you understand your project and can tell them about it clearly and thoroughly. Good luck!

Name _____ Date _____

**Decide whether each statement is true or false.
Circle *T* or *F* at the right of each statement.**

1. Lightning is an example of static electricity.   1.   T   F

2. Current flows easily through an insulator.   2.   T   F

3. Copper is a good insulator.   3.   T   F

4. The diagram shows a series circuit.   4.   T   F

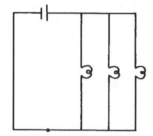

5. In a magnet, two like poles repel each other.   5.   T   F

**Read each question. Choose the best answer from those
listed. Write the letter of your choice on the line at the right.**

6. Static electricity is produced when   6. _____
   a. objects lose all their charges.
   b. negative charges become positive charges.
   c. negative charges move from one object to another.
   d. positive charges move from one object to another.

7. If one of the lights goes out in a series   7. _____
   circuit, the others will
   a. go out.
   b. become brighter.
   c. become dimmer.
   d. remain the same.

GO ON TO THE NEXT PAGE ▶

Unit 1 Assessment

Name _____ Date _____

8. The ends of a magnet are called
   a. the poles.
   b. the lines of force.
   c. a magnetic field.
   d. a magnetic force.

8. _____

9. The difference between electromagnets and regular magnets is that electromagnets
   a. have a magnetic force.
   b. can be turned on and off.
   c. attract different materials.
   d. have north and south poles.

9. _____

10. A piece of iron with wire wrapped around it becomes an electromagnet when
   a. it is in a magnetic field.
   b. the iron is in a north-south direction.
   c. the wire touches a magnet.
   d. a current is passed through the wire.

10. _____

11. How does increasing the amount of current affect an electromagnet?
   a. It becomes weaker.
   b. It becomes stronger.
   c. The direction of the poles is reversed.
   d. It has no effect.

11. _____

Use the drawings to answer question 12.

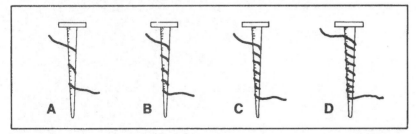

12. Which electromagnet will pick up the most nails?
   a. A   **b.** B   **c.** C   **d.** D

12. _____

Unit 2 Assessment

**Decide whether each statement is true or false.
Circle *T* or *F* at the right of each statement.**

---

1. Motion is described by comparing a moving object
   to a reference point.   **1.**   T   F

2. Speed is calculated by multiplying the distance
   traveled by the travel time.   **2.**   T   F

3. Friction is a force that resists movement.   **3.**   T   F

4. Objects in motion tend to keep moving unless some
   force acts on them to stop them.   **4.**   T   F

5. A car can accelerate by changing its speed.   **5.**   T   F

**Read each question. Choose the best answer from those
listed. Write the letter of your choice on the line at the right.**

---

6. When you compare the position of a moving bicycle   **6.** _____
   to the sidewalk, you are describing the bicycle's
   a. speed.
   b. motion.
   c. velocity.
   d. acceleration.

7. The force that pulls things toward each other is called **7.** _____
   a. friction.
   b. mass.
   c. motion.
   d. gravity.

GO ON TO THE NEXT PAGE ➤

Unit 2 Assessment, p. 2

8. The speed of a car that travels 150 kilometers in 3 hours is
   a. 50 kph.   b. 450 kph.
   c. 75 kph.   d. 55 kph.

8. _____

9. In what way is friction useful to a skydiver?
   a. It speeds up the fall.
   b. It slows down the fall.
   c. It holds air in the parachute.
   d. It increases the pull of gravity.

9. _____

10. The amount of inertia an object has depends on its
    a. mass.   b. speed.
    c. motion. d. size.

10. _____

11. The scientist who first stated the laws of motion was
    a. Einstein.   b. Galileo.
    c. Newton.   d. Fermi.

11. _____

12. Which of the following is an example of accelerated motion?
    a. an airplane traveling at a constant speed
    b. a sled gaining speed as it goes downhill
    c. a car parked on a hill
    d. a bicycle going 30 kph on a level road

12. _____

13. A force of gravity opposes the force of
    a. friction.   b. inertia.
    c. energy.   d. acceleration.

13. _____

14. The action and reaction forces are equal when a basketball is
    a. resting on the floor.   b. falling through the hoop.
    c. being dribbled.   d. passed from one player to another.

14. _____

Unit 2 Assessment

Name _____   Date _____

Unit 3 Assessment

Decide whether each statement is true or false. Circle *T* or *F* at the right of each statement.

1. A balance is used to measure mass.   1.   T   F

2. Matter can be described by properties of color and taste.   2.   T   F

3. Gas molecules only move by vibrating.   3.   T   F

4. The weight in a substance decreases after a chemical reaction. 4.   T   F

5. Cutting paper is an example of a physical change.   5.   T   F

Read each question. Choose the best answer from those listed. Write the letter of your choice on the line at the right.

6. Water can change into a gas through   6. _____
   a. condensation.
   b. evaporation.
   c. chemical change.
   d. cooling.

7. Water is   7. _____
   a. an element.
   b. a compound.
   c. a solution.
   d. an atom.

GO ON TO THE NEXT PAGE ➤

Unit 3 Assessment

Unit 3 Assessment, p. 2

8. Since lemon juice is an acid, it will change   8. _____
  a. blue litmus paper to pink.
  b. pink litmus paper to blue.
  c. blue litmus paper to purple.
  d. pink litmus paper to purple.

9. Hydrogen and oxygen make   9. _____
  a. carbon dioxide.   **b.** hydrogen peroxide.
  c. mercuric oxide.   **d.** water.

10. An example of a chemical reaction is   10. _____
  a. a burning fire.
  b. a reaction between baking soda and vinegar.
  c. rusting iron.
  d. all of the above.

11. When two substances go through a chemical change,   11. _____
  a. they always turn into gases.
  b. their physical properties remain the same.
  c. their molecules remain the same.
  d. they form a new substance with different properties.

12. The smallest part of a substance that has all the   12. _____
  properties of that substance is
  a. a base.   **b.** a molecule.
  c. an atom.   **d.** an acid.

13. The chemical formula that shows three hydrogen   13. _____
  atoms combined with one nitrogen atom is
  a. $(NH)_3$.   **b.** $_3NH$.
  c. N_3H_1.   **d.** NH_3.

14. Lemonade is an example of a   14. _____
  a. colloid.   **b.** compound.
  c. solution.   **d.** molecule.

Unit 1 A Charge for Life

INTRODUCTION

The world is quickly changing. The use of electric energy has made these changes and advances in technology possible. This unit will explore static and current electricity. Students will learn about different kinds of circuits and how energy travels through them. Students will then examine the energy of magnets and how electric energy can be transferred into magnetism. Finally, students will review safety procedures when near electric sources and the reasons for this caution.

ELECTRIC ENERGY

Electric energy is a form of energy that creates a force, a push or pull, that causes other objects to move. It is the result of a negative charge when electrons move away from an object or are pushed along a path producing a negative charge. This movement can then be transferred into heat, sound, light, or other kinds of movement.

Static Electricity

Matter is made of tiny particles called *atoms*. Atoms are composed of protons, electrons, and neutrons. Protons have positive charges, electrons have negative charges, and neutrons have no charge. Protons and neutrons are inside the nucleus of an atom, while electrons orbit around it. If a particle has the same number of positive and negative charges, there is no charge—it is called neutral. Most matter has a neutral charge.

A neutral object can lose electrons when it is rubbed. The charges move in all directions. The negative charges jump to other objects, creating static electricity. Objects that have static electricity attract objects that have opposite charges. They repulse those that have the same kind of charge. Sometimes, a plastic comb will create static electricity as the hair is brushed. Negative charges from the comb jump to the hair. Since each hair is similarly charged, it repulses the other strands of hair. Sometimes, light objects that have a neutral charge even attract objects with static electricity.

Lightning is another example of static electricity. Extra electrons build up in clouds. As millions of the electrons jump from cloud to cloud, lightning is produced. Lightning strikes materials that conduct electricity, such as metal and water. For these reasons, it is unsafe to be near water or to use the telephone during an electric storm. Lightning also strikes tall objects. If you are caught in a storm, it is unwise to stand under a tree, since lightning would be more likely to strike it. Moreover, the body is a good conductor. A lightning strike in a tree could jump to a person's body.

Current Electricity

Electricity gives us light, sound, heat, and movement. It is caused by matter that has an electric charge—a negative charge. In electricity the matter is negatively charged and moves in the same direction. By moving in one direction, the charge makes a current. The rate that the current flows depends on the number of charges and how much the wire resists the current. *Amperes* is the scientific unit that measures the amount of electrons moving past a point in a given interval of time.

Most electricity is made by generators. Generators push the charged particles in the same direction through a conductor. A *conductor* is a material that charged particles can move through easily. Wires are the main source of movement. Water is another material that conducts an electric current. Any material that a current cannot pass through, such as rubber, is an *insulator.* Rubber generally covers wires to keep the charges moving in one direction. Without the insulator, wires would heat, and the moving energy would be lost.

Electricity is measured in watts. Electric usage is measured in kilowatt-hours. An average of 1,000 kilowatts is used in an hour. Meters on buildings count the number of kilowatt-hours used. They are generally read once each month.

Dry Cells

Dry cells, often used in energy experiments, store electric energy. The inside of a dry cell is made of chemicals that create a chemical reaction with the mineral zinc. An electric current is formed. A dry cell has terminals at the top: one holds a positive charge, and the other holds a negative charge. When wires are attached from each terminal to a source that uses an electric charge, a closed circuit is formed. Batteries are similar to dry cells but can hold more charges than a dry cell.

CIRCUITS

A circuit is the path an electric current travels. There are four parts in a circuit: the source, path, switch, and resistor. The charge leaves the energy source, such as a battery or outlet, and moves through a wire to the resistor, which uses the electric charge, such as a light bulb or toaster. It then must follow a separate path back to its source. The switch controls when the electrons flow. If the charge does not return to its original source, the charge builds up, causing the circuit not to work, or to short.

When the circuit is completed, it is called a closed circuit. An open circuit is one in which a part of the path is missing. The charge is unable to follow its complete path. When a switch is off, the circuit is opened; the electric current does not flow. When the switch is on, the circuit is closed, and the current is able to flow.

Series Circuit

A series circuit is made when all parts of the circuit are joined one after the other. The electric current flows in one path. If one part of the circuit is open or broken, the current does not flow to all the other parts. Many resistors may be added to a series circuit. However, the amount of energy flowing through the wires is the same. The resistors must share the available current. The result is that the users may not work to full capacity. For example, if there are three light bulbs on a series circuit, all the bulbs will be dimmer than if only one bulb serves as a resistor.

Parallel Circuit

A parallel circuit has more than one path that an electric current can travel. Several resistors are placed on separate paths and are independent of the others. If one resistor is broken or the circuit is open, the others still operate. The current flow increases when there are more paths. If there are too many paths, it is possible for them to overheat and melt, resulting in a fire. Fuses reduce the risk of this hazard in parallel circuits. A fuse is a piece of wire that melts when it gets too hot. When it melts, the circuit opens, and the flow of electricity stops. Circuit breakers also serve as a safety device. They open the circuit to break the flow of electricity.

MAGNETISM

Magnetism is a force that attracts metal materials, like iron, steel, nickel, and cobalt. The force is found naturally in lodestone rock. Magnets attract, or pull, and repel, or push, other pieces of metal. Synthetic magnets are made from steel or a combination of aluminum, nickel, cobalt, and iron. It is easy to transfer a magnetic charge to iron, but the charge will not last. Proper storage of synthetic magnets is important for them to retain their force.

Magnets come in all shapes and sizes. The force is focused at the ends, or poles, of the magnets. These poles have a north and a south side. Most magnets are marked with an *N* and an *S* to identify the poles. (However, if they are not marked on a bar magnet, hang the magnet from a string. The north end of the magnet will point toward the north.) Like ends of two magnets repel each other. In other words, if two north ends of magnets are held together, they will repel each other. Unlike ends, a south and a north end, attract each other. The area between the poles has some magnetic force, too, but it is not as strong as the poles.

Magnets do not need to touch, though. There is a magnetic force around each magnet called a magnetic field. When a piece of metal comes within a certain distance of the magnet, the magnet's field starts to pull the metal. The pull increases as the metal gets closer to the magnet. The size of the magnet affects the strength of the magnetic field.

Magnets can also produce an electric charge. When moved back and forth inside a metal coil, magnets produce electricity. Generators were developed based on this principle. They create electricity by moving either a coil of wire through a magnetic field or by moving a magnet through wire coils.

Electromagnets

As electric charges move through a wire, a magnetic field is created around the wire. It is this force that is used to make an electromagnet. A metal bar is wrapped in wire and connected to an electric source, such as a dry cell. The more wire used, the greater the magnetic field and the stronger the magnet will be. Electromagnets have switches so the magnetic field can be turned on and off. Doorbells and cranes in junkyards use the energy of electromagnets.

Galvanometer

A galvanometer is a device that can measure weak amounts of electric current. Coils of wire are connected to a free-floating magnet, similar to a compass. The needle moves when placed near a current.

SAFETY

Safety precautions should be taken when you are around electric devices. All outlets carry electricity. Anything put into a receptacle can transfer the electrical current to the object. Appliances that are not in use should be unplugged. Only plugs of mechanically safe appliances should be plugged into an outlet. Empty outlets should be covered with safety caps.

Since water is a good conductor of electricity, all electrical appliances need to be kept away from water, including rain. An electric shock is the result when water and electricity interact. The contact could result in immediate death. Electricity is an important part of life, but it can be dangerous if care is not taken.

Electric Charges

Have you ever rubbed a balloon on your shirt or your hair and then put it on the wall? Why does it stick? The reason is because of electric charges. Every object has electric charges, but they are too small to see. There are two kinds of charges—positive charges and negative charges. Objects that have more negative charges than positive charges are negatively charged. Objects that have more positive charges than negative charges are positively charged.

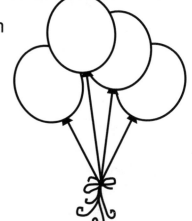

Positively charged objects attract negatively charged objects and repel other positively charged objects. Negatively charged objects attract positively charged objects and repel other negatively charged objects.

Underline the best answer.

1. If you rub a balloon on your shirt or in your hair and then touch it to the wall, it will . . .

    a. stick to the wall.   **b.** fall to the floor.

    c. roll up to the ceiling.   **d.** push away from the wall.

2. If pieces of confetti will stick to a balloon, then you know that the balloon is . . .

    a. sticky.   **b.** charged.

    c. uncharged.   **d.** filled with helium.

3. An object that has more negative charges than positive charges is . . .

    a. uncharged.   **b.** neutral.

    c. positively charged.   **d.** negatively charged.

4. If two balloons are both negatively charged, they will . . .

    a. attract each other.   **b.** repel each other.

    c. stick to each other.   **d.** be neutral.

Name _____   Date _____

Static Electricity

All matter contains a positive or negative charge. Negative charges can move from one object to another. Static electricity results when an object gains or loses a charge. The objects may attract or repel each other. If they attract, they pull together. If they repel, they push apart. Objects with like charges repel each other, while those with opposite charges attract each other.

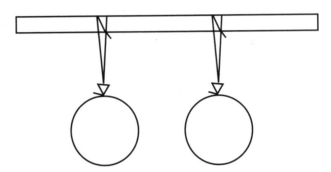

 Answer the questions.

1. What would happen if each balloon were given a positive charge?

_____

_____

2. What would happen if each balloon were given a negative charge?

_____

_____

3. What would happen if one balloon were given a positive charge and the other a negative charge?

_____

_____

4. What happens if hair has static electricity?

_____

_____

_____

Name _____ Date _____

How Can You Produce Static Electricity?

Electricity is a form of energy that causes movement. A force, a push or pull, causes this movement. Particles of negatively charged matter move from one object to another, resulting in one object that has a positive charge and another with a negative charge.

✔ **You will need:**

| 1 sheet of paper | wool cloth |
| plastic ruler | wooden pencil shavings |

1. Tear the paper into small pieces.

2. Rub the wool cloth quickly up and down the plastic ruler.

3. Hold the ruler about 2 cm above the torn paper pieces. What happens? Record your observations on the table below.

4. Hold the ruler about 2 cm above the pencil shavings. What happens? Record your observations on the table below.

Static Electricity

Object	Reaction Observed
Pieces of paper	
Wood shavings	

GO ON TO THE NEXT PAGE ➤

Unit 1: A Charge for Life

How Can You Produce Static Electricity?, p. 2

Answer the questions.

1. What happened when you brought the ruler near the pieces of paper?

   _____

   _____

2. What happened when you brought the ruler near the wood shavings?

   _____

   _____

3. How did you know that a static charge was produced?

   _____

   _____

4. When you rubbed the ruler with the wool cloth, which object received extra negative charges?

   _____

   _____

5. When you brought the ruler near the paper and the wood shavings, what happened to some of their negative charges?

   _____

   _____

Lightning Is Electricity

Ben Franklin proved lightning was electricity striking the Earth when he did his kite flying experiment. As a result of this experiment, Franklin invented the lightning rod. The lightning rod is a metal stick placed high on buildings. Lightning will strike objects that are good conductors of electricity, such as water and metal. Lightning usually strikes the highest object around. The lightning rod is the highest object on a building. It is made of metal to attract lightning to it. This prevents the building itself from getting struck.

But even Benjamin Franklin misjudged the power of lightning. He did not think a man could have been harmed by touching a lightning rod. Today, we know Benjamin Franklin was lucky he was not killed.

Here are some do's and don'ts in a thunderstorm. Next to each rule, write a sentence to explain why following these rules will reduce the chances of getting struck by lightning.

Lightning Do's

1. Go indoors _____

_____

2. Put golf clubs away _____

_____

GO ON TO THE NEXT PAGE ▶

Unit 1: A Charge for Life

Lightning Is Electricity, p. 2

3. Stay in your car _____

_____

4. Sit down low outdoors _____

_____

5. Stay off the telephone _____

_____

Lightning Don'ts

6. Walk on hilltops _____

_____

7. Go under a tree _____

_____

8. Swim _____

_____

9. Climb rock ledges _____

_____

Unit 1: A Charge for Life

Circuits

Charges do not always stay in one place. In fact, they can move very well through some materials. For example, you can use copper wires to connect a light bulb to a battery so that charges flow out of one end of the battery, through the light bulb, and into the other end of the battery. The loop made by the battery, wires, and light bulb is called a *circuit*. The flow of charges through the circuit is called *current electricity*. When the circuit is complete, or closed, the charges can travel all the way through it and will light the bulb. If the circuit is incomplete, or open, then the bulb will not light. A switch can be added to open and close the circuit so the light bulb can be turned on and off.

There is only one way to wire a circuit with just one light bulb and one battery. But if you add another light bulb, there are two ways to wire them together. In a series circuit, all of the electric charges travel first through one of the light bulbs and then through the other one. In a parallel circuit, there are two paths for the charges to follow. Some travel through one path to one of the light bulbs, while the rest travel through the other path to the other light bulb.

Underline the best answer.

1. Electric charges do not flow all the way through . . .
   a. an open circuit.   **b.** a closed circuit.
   c. a wire.   **d.** a battery.

2. If you remove the bulb from a circuit, the current will . . .
   a. get brighter.   **b.** get faster.
   c. get dimmer.   **d.** go out.

3. For a circuit to work, the part not needed is the . . .
   a. wires.   **b.** switch.
   c. battery.   **d.** light bulb.

Unit 1: A Charge for Life

Making an Electric Switch

When a switch is closed (or on), a circuit is completed. Electric current can pass through. When a switch is open (or off), the circuit is broken and the electric current cannot flow.

> ✔ **You will need:**
>
> | | |
> |---|---|
> | 2 steel thumbtacks | 1.5 volt dry cell |
> | tin snips | wire cutters |
> | 3 strips of insulated wire | tin can |
> | light bulb and bulb holder | hammer |
> | piece of wood, 12 cm X 8 cm | metric ruler |

1. Strip about 1 cm of insulation from the ends of all the wires.

2. Have your teacher cut a 6 cm X 2 cm strip of metal from the tin can and bend it to form an *S*. Caution: Be careful when handling the metal strip. The edges may be sharp.

3. Connect two wires to the bulb holder. Make a loop at the end of one of these wires. Place a tack through the loop and hammer it into the wood.

4. Attach the other wire from the bulb holder to one terminal of the dry cell.

5. Loop one end of the remaining wire around the second tack. Hammer the tack through one end of the metal strip and into the wood. It should be placed about 4 cm from the first tack.

6. Connect the other end of the remaining wire to the dry cell. To complete the circuit, turn on your switch. Just press down on the metal strip. Be sure the strip touches the tack.

What happens? _____

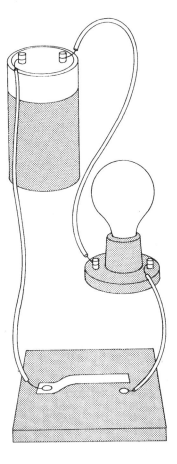

Unit 1: A Charge for Life
Physical Science 5, SV 3764-X

Name _____ Date _____

Is It a Conductor or an Insulator?

A conductor is a material that allows a current to flow through it easily, such as metal. An insulator is a material that keeps a current from moving through it, such as rubber or plastic.

✔ **You will need:**

3 pieces of insulated copper wire, each 30 cm long
and stripped to 2.5 cm on each end
light bulb in socket   D-size battery   screwdriver
sheet of aluminum foil   door key   sheet of paper
penny   rubber band
pencil, sharpened on each end

1. Look at the table on page 28. Read the list of objects in the *Item Tested* column. Predict which items are insulators and which are conductors. Record your predictions.

2. Connect the 3 pieces of wire, light bulb, and battery as shown in the picture.

3. Hold the uncovered ends of the 2 wires to the foil. Watch what happens.

4. Record your observation on the table on page 28.

5. Repeat Steps 3 and 4 for each item listed on the table.

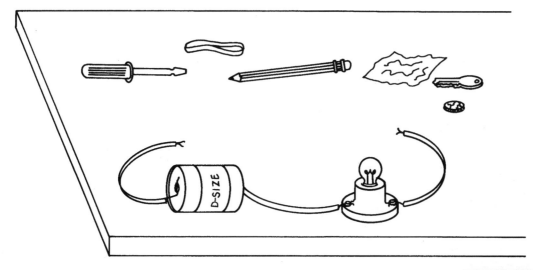

GO ON TO THE NEXT PAGE ➤

Name _____   Date _____

Is It a Conductor or an Insulator?, p. 2

Conductors and Insulators

Item Tested	Prediction	Conductor	Insulator
Aluminum foil			
Door key			
Paper			
Penny			
Rubber band			
Pencil			

Answer the questions.

1. Which items were conductors?

_____

_____

2. Which items were insulators?

_____

_____

3. Which of your predictions were correct? Which were not correct?

_____

_____

4. What kinds of materials make good conductors?

_____

_____

How Can You Make a Series Circuit?

A resistor is a device that uses the electrical energy because it resists the flow of energy. A light bulb is an example of a resistor. When a circuit has two or more resistors and the electrical current flows in one direction, then it is called a series circuit. In this kind of circuit, the flow of electricity stays the same. The resistors must share the flow, so they may not be able to work to full capacity.

You will need:

4 pieces of insulated copper wire, each 30 cm long and stripped to 2.5 cm on each end

1.5 volt dry cell   2 light bulbs in sockets
screwdriver   switch

1. Connect a series circuit with wires as follows:
- join one terminal of the dry cell to one light bulb
- join the first light bulb to the second one
- join the second light bulb to the switch
- join the switch to the remaining dry cell terminal.

2. Close the switch, then open it. What happened?

3. Unscrew one light bulb. What do you think will happen?

4. Close the switch, then open it. What happened?

GO ON TO THE NEXT PAGE ▶

Unit 1: A Charge for Life
Physical Science 5, SV 3764-X

How Can You Make a Series Circuit?, p. 2

Answer the questions.

1. What happened when you closed the switch the first time?

_____

_____

_____

2. What happened when you closed the switch after you unscrewed one light bulb?

_____

_____

_____

3. Through how many paths can an electric current flow in a series circuit? How do you know?

_____

_____

_____

4. Write two hypotheses for this activity. Each one should begin with the word *If* and have the word *then* in it.

_____

_____

_____

_____

_____

Unit 1: A Charge for Life

How Can You Make a Parallel Circuit?

A parallel circuit has more than one path that an electric current can travel through. These circuits usually have a fuse or circuit breaker joined to them to keep the wires from getting too hot.

✔ **You will need:**

1.5 volt dry cell	3 light bulbs in sockets
switch	screwdriver

7 pieces of insulated copper wire, each 30 cm long and stripped to 2.5 cm on each end

1. Connect a parallel circuit with wires as follows:
- join one terminal of the dry cell to one light bulb
- join the first light bulb to the second bulb
- join the second light bulb to the third bulb
- join the bulbs in the reverse order to the switch
- join the switch to the remaining dry cell terminal.

2. Close the switch, then open it. What happened?

3. Unscrew one light bulb. What do you think will happen?

4. Close the switch, then open it. What happened?

GO ON TO THE NEXT PAGE ➤

How Can You Make a Parallel Circuit?, p. 2

Answer the questions.

1. What happened when you closed the switch the first time?

_____

_____

2. What happened when you closed the switch the second time?

_____

_____

3. Through how many paths can an electric current flow in a parallel circuit? How do you know?

_____

_____

4. What is the difference between a series circuit and a parallel circuit?

_____

_____

_____

Unit 1: A Charge for Life

Physical Science 5, SV 3764-X

Circuit Diagrams

In each space below, draw a diagram of the circuit described using the symbols given on the chart. The first one is done for you.

1. A series circuit with 1 dry cell, 2 light bulbs, and an open switch.

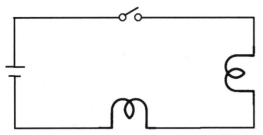

2. A parallel circuit with 2 dry cells, 3 light bulbs, and a closed switch.

3. A series circuit with 2 dry cells, 4 light bulbs, and a closed switch.

4. A parallel circuit with 1 dry cell, 2 light bulbs, and an open switch.

Chart of electrical symbols		
	Circuit part	**Symbol**
dry cell		
light bulb		
open switch		
closed switch		
wire		
fuse		
broken fuse		

Unit 1: A Charge for Life
Physical Science 5, SV 3764-X

What Would Happen?

Explain what would happen in the examples given below.

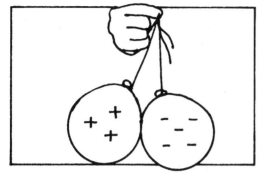

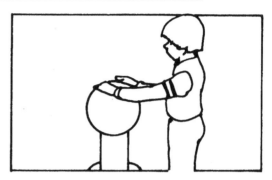

1. _____   2. _____

_____   _____

_____   _____

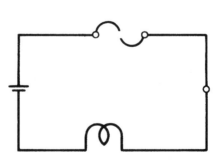

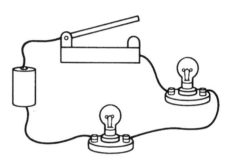

3. _____   4. _____

_____   _____

_____   _____

5. _____   6. _____

_____   _____

_____   _____

Name _____   Date _____

Electricity

As electric current flows, wires and other objects in the circuit may get too hot. They can cause the circuit to short and change the flow of electricity. A fuse is made with a wire that melts if the current gets too hot.

You will need:

| aluminum foil | 2 dry cells | 2 paper clips | scissors |
| ruler | 2 thumbtacks | wire | wooden block |
| screwdriver with insulated handle |

SAFETY TIP: THIS ACTIVITY MUST BE SUPERVISED BY AN ADULT.

1. Place each paper clip against the underside of a thumbtack. Press the thumbtacks into the wooden block as shown. The tacks should be about 3 cm apart and upright against the wood.

2. Place a strip of aluminum foil about 5 cm long by 1 cm wide between the clips.

3. Set up the dry cells, wire, and bulb as shown.

4. Remove some insulation near the middle of the wires as shown.

5. While holding the insulated handle of the screwdriver, carefully touch the metal to the two stripped wires. Observe what happens to the aluminum.

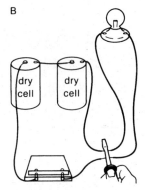

Answer the questions.

1. How did you short the circuit? _____

2. Did the current travel back to the source through the bulb or the screwdriver? _____

3. What happened to the foil? Why? _____

_____

4. Why is a fuse helpful in a circuit? _____

_____

Unit 1: A Charge for Life

How Does a Flashlight Work?

A flashlight is a handy item to have if the lights go out. You have probably used a flashlight, but have you ever studied its parts? This activity will help you understand how a flashlight works. You will need a working flashlight with a plastic case that uses D dry cells. Carefully take the flashlight apart. Take apart the section that has the dry cells and the section that has the bulb. Leave the switch in place. Draw what you see.

Answer the questions.

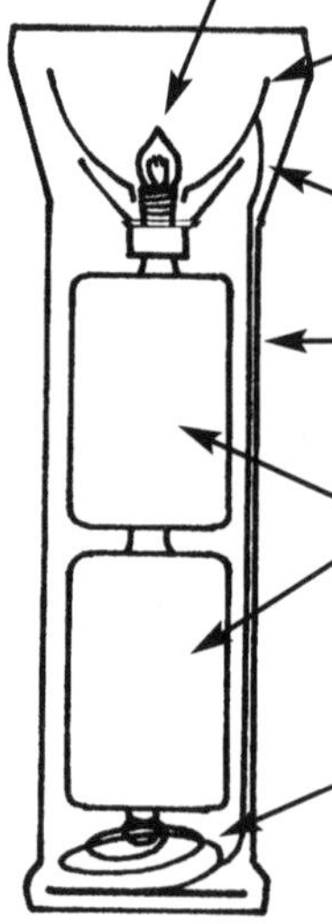

1. Compare your drawing of the flashlight with this labeled drawing. Are there any parts that are different? _____

   _____

2. Why are there no wires except for a small wire under the bottom battery? _____

   _____

3. Make a hypothesis about how the switch in your flashlight permits current to flow or stops the flow of current.

   _____

   _____

   _____

4. Describe the path that charges take in a flashlight.

   _____

   _____

   _____

   _____

bulb

metal reflector

metal strip

switch

dry cells

spring

Unit 1: A Charge for Life

Making a Magnet

Magnets attract objects made of iron, nickel, and cobalt. The forces are strongest at their poles, or ends. Some metals can become like a magnet.

☑ **You will need:**

bar magnet	candle with holder
hammer	3 iron nails
matches	paper clips
pliers	

NOTE: THIS ACTIVITY MUST BE SUPERVISED BY AN ADULT.

1. Stroke one of the iron nails with the pole of the magnet in one direction only.

2. Try to pick up the paper clips with the nail.

3. Remove the clips. Then hammer along the length of the nail several times. Try to pick up the clips again.

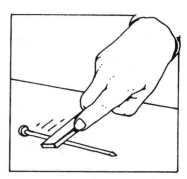

4. Repeat Step 1 with another nail. Remove the clips.

5. Stroke the nail with the pole of the magnet in both directions. Try to pick up the clips again.

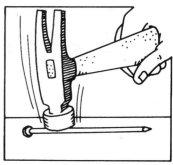

6. Repeat Step 1 with another nail. Then remove the clips.

7. Hold the nail with the pliers and place the nail in the flame of a candle for about three minutes. Try to pick up the clips again.

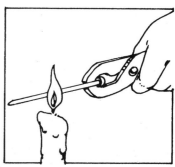

GO ON TO THE NEXT PAGE ➤

Unit 1: A Charge for Life

Making a Magnet, p. 2

1. How did you make the nails act like magnets?

_____

_____

_____

2. What happened to the nails after you hammered or heated them?

_____

_____

3. What happened to the nail after rubbing it with the magnet in both directions? _____

_____

4. What are three ways in which magnetism can be destroyed?

_____

_____

Magnetic Force

Each end of a magnet is called a *pole.* There is a north pole, labeled *N,* and a south pole, labeled *S.* The magnetic force is strongest at the poles. The poles have different forces. If you put the ends of the poles of two magnets close to each other, the magnets will either push away from each other or pull toward each other. If the magnets pull together, the poles are unlike poles. If they push apart, the poles are like poles.

Below are drawings of magnets. On each, draw the lines of force that show the location of the magnetic field.

1.
N	S

2.
S	N		N	S

3.
S	N		S	N

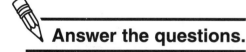

Answer the questions.

4. What do the letters *N* and *S* stand for on the magnets?

_____

5. How could you test each of the predictions you have made?

_____

_____

_____

How Can You See the Effect of a Magnetic Field?

The space around the magnet is the magnetic field. The force is strongest around the poles of the magnets.

You will need:

metal filings (or a steel wool pad cut into small pieces)
bar magnet   plastic cup   sheet of plastic

1. Place the bar magnet on the table. Cover it with the sheet of plastic.

2. Sprinkle the iron filings on the plastic sheet on the magnet.

3. Gently tap the edge of the sheet.

4. Draw what you see in the space below.

Answer the questions.

1. What is a magnetic field? _____

_____

2. What parts of the magnet have the strongest magnetic field?

_____

Unit 1: A Charge for Life

Name _____   Date _____

How Do Nonmagnetic Materials Affect a Magnet?

Materials made of metal, such as iron, nickel, and cobalt, are attracted by a magnet. In this activity, you will find out if nonmagnetic materials affect a magnetic field.

 You will need:

alnico magnet	a paper clip	string 37 cm (15 in.) long
block of wood	squares of paper	aluminum foil
cloth	waxed paper	iron nail
ring stand with test-tube holder		

1. Set up the materials as shown in the drawing.

2. Pass the squares of paper through the space between the clip and the pole of the magnet. Record your results on the table.

3. Pass the foil, cloth, waxed paper, and nail through the space.

4. Repeat the experiment with the poles reversed.

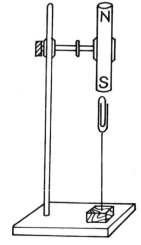

Answer the questions.

1. Why is the paper clip held in place? _____

   _____

2. What happened in Step 2? Explain. _____

   _____

3. Did any of the materials affect the magnetic field? Why? _____

   _____

4. What happened when you reversed the bar magnet so the *N* pole pointed down? Explain.

   _____

Magnetic Attraction	
Material	**Effect**
paper	
foil	
cloth	
waxed paper	
nail	

Electromagnets

Electromagnets are made by wrapping wire around a long piece of iron. An electric current travels through the wire and causes the iron to become magnetized. The iron loses its magnetic force when the current is turned off. The magnetic field is stronger when more wire is wrapped around the metal or a stronger current travels through the wire.

a.
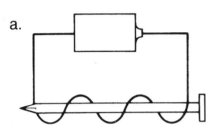

b.
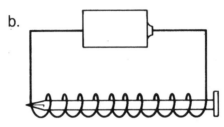

c.
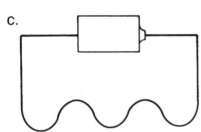

d.
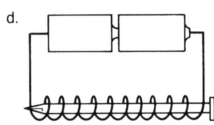

1. Arrange the letters of the electromagnets in order of increasing strength.

_____

2. Many devices use electromagnets, such as telephones and cranes that move metal. Choose a device and research to find how it uses an electromagnet. Write a brief explanation below.

_____

_____

_____

_____

_____

_____

_____

Name _____   Date _____

How Does a Telegraph Work?

A telegraph is a device that sends messages in code. It uses both electricity and magnetism.

✔ **You will need:**

1 dry cell	2 thin iron or steel strips
large-headed nail	2 long nails
4 small nails	wire
wood block	wood board

1. Hammer the large-headed nail into the center of the board.

2. Nail one metal strip near one end of the board as shown. Bend the strip back so that it does not touch the board when you let it go.

3. Hammer a small nail into the wood under the end of the metal strip.

4. Attach a wire from this small nail to the dry cell. Attach the other wire to the dry cell. Then wrap the wire around the large nail about 40 times. Attach the loose end of the wire to the nail in the metal strip.

5. Hammer the block into the other end of the wood. Nail a metal strip to the top of the block so the strip reaches over the large nail. Bend the strip down at the center and up at the end.

6. Press down and release the key.

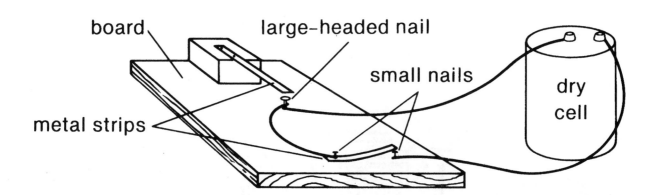

board   large-headed nail
small nails
dry cell
metal strips

GO ON TO THE NEXT PAGE ➡

Unit 1: A Charge for Life

How Does a Telegraph Work?, p.2

Answer the questions.

1. What happened when you pressed down on the key?

_____

2. What part is the electromagnet?

_____

_____

3. How is the circuit closed?

_____

_____

4. A telegraph uses electricity to make sounds. How is the sound made?

_____

_____

_____

_____

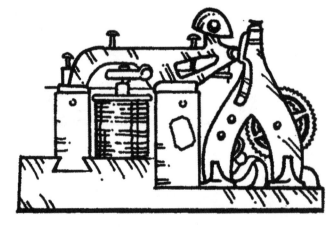

Unit 1: A Charge for Life

How We Use Electromagnets

Unlike permanent magnets, electromagnets work only when electric current is running through them. That makes them very useful. For example, think about a huge magnet on a crane in a scrap yard. It separates the iron from the other metals. The crane's magnet can pick up a load of iron from the scrap because the iron sticks to the magnet. Because the magnet is an electromagnet, though, it can be switched off. So, in a scrap yard, the crane operator lifts the scrap iron to the place he or she wants it and then turns off the magnet. The load of iron falls into a pile below.

We use electromagnets every day. When the doorbell rings, an electromagnet is at work. When you use a telephone, you are using an electromagnet. Motors use electromagnets. So do toasters. Here are diagrams of two electromagnets people use every day.

Iron is pulled toward electromagnet

Hammer hits gong

Wires to doorbell, button, and electrical source

When someone pushes a doorbell, an electric current is switched on. An electromagnet inside the doorbell becomes magnetized and attracts a piece of iron. The iron moves toward the electromagnet. A hammer attached to the piece of iron hits the bell and it rings.

GO ON TO THE NEXT PAGE ▶

How We Use Electromagnets, p. 2

When someone starts a car, this is what happens: The driver turns the key. That creates a small electric current. The current causes an electromagnet to move toward another magnet and hit a switch. That switch starts the engine.

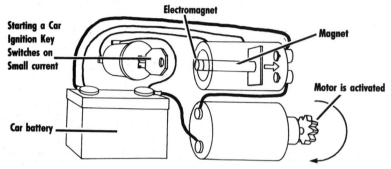

Answer the questions.

1. What would happen if the magnet in the scrap yard were a permanent magnet instead of an electromagnet?

_____

_____

2. What does the iron do in the doorbell?

_____

_____

3. Why is it important to have an electromagnet rather than a permanent magnet in a doorbell?

_____

_____

4. Why is the key important in the car's starter?

_____

_____

How Can You Make a Galvanometer?

Magnets inside coils of wire can produce an electric current. A galvanometer is a device that can measure the weak electric currents the magnets make.

✔ You will need:
bar magnet
2 pieces of wire, 90 cm long
cardboard tube
compass

1. Wrap one piece of wire around the cardboard tube. Leave about 15 cm of wire free on each end.

2. Wrap the other piece of wire around the compass front to back. Make sure you can still see the compass needle. Leave about 30 cm of wire free on each end.

3. Connect the ends of the wires of the tube to the ends of the wires of the compass.

4. Carefully slide the tube out of the coil of wire.

5. Move the magnet back and forth inside the coil of wire. Watch the compass needle.

6. Hold the magnet still. Watch the compass needle.

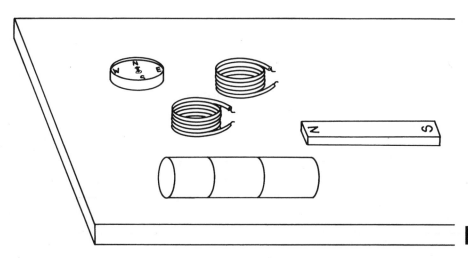

Name _____   Date _____

How Can You Make a Galvanometer?, p. 2

Answer the questions.

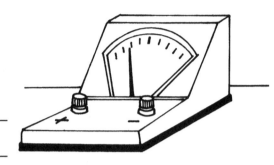

1. What happened to the compass needle when you moved the magnet?

   _____

   _____

2. What happened when you held the magnet still?

   _____

   _____

   _____

3. When was the bar magnet producing an electric current? How do you know? _____

   _____

   _____

4. What part of the setup is the galvanometer?

   _____

   _____

   _____

5. The discovery that magnets could produce electric current led to the invention of generators. Research generators and how they use magnetism.

   _____

   _____

   _____

   _____

The Compass

It is thought that the Earth's interior acts something like a bar magnet. This gives the Earth north and south magnetic poles. A magnetic field originates at the poles and surrounds the Earth. This magnetic field has been detected by astronauts in space. They floated magnets in their space capsules and found these magnets moved to stay in line with the Earth's magnetic field. On the Earth, a compass with a magnetized needle also lines up with the Earth's magnetic field.

You will need:

clear plastic cup no larger than 6 cm on the bottom
sewing needle   large index card   clock
paste   strong magnet

1. Cut out the compass circle below and paste it to the index card.

2. To make the needle a magnet, lay the needle on the magnet. Leave it there for 30 minutes. Remove the needle from the magnet by lifting it straight up.

3. Fill the cup with water and carefully lay the magnetized needle on the surface of the water. Turn the cup until the needle points to north on the compass circle. Paste the cup to the circle.

Answer the questions.

1. Does your compass point north? _____

2. Would this compass work on the Moon? Why or why not? _____

_____

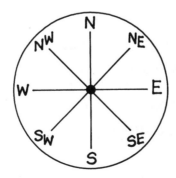

Unit 1: A Charge for Life
Physical Science 5, SV 3764-X

Name _____ Date _____

How Are Kilowatt-Hours Measured?

Electricity is measured in watts. A watt is a unit that measures how much electricity is needed to run an appliance. A kilowatt is a larger unit of measure that equals 1,000 watts. If an appliance uses 1,000 watts for an hour, it uses a kilowatt-hour of electricity.

 You will need:
electric meter

1. Find an electric meter. Read the number on it in the morning.

2. Record the number in the second row on the table below.

3. On the following morning, read the number on the meter again.

4. Record the number in the first row on the table below.

5. Subtract the smaller number from the larger number. The difference is the number of kilowatt-hours used. Record the difference on the table.

Meter Reading

Meter Reading	Number
Kilowatt-hours on second reading	
Kilowatt-hours on first reading	
Kilowatt-hours used	

Answer the questions.

1. If you used the same number of kilowatt-hours for one 30-day month, how many kilowatt-hours would you use? _____

2. Suppose a kilowatt-hour costs 10 cents. How much would you pay to the electric company for the month? _____

Unit 1: A Charge for Life
Physical Science 5, SV 3764-X

Conserving Electricity

Some electric power is produced by burning fossil fuels, such as coal and gas. Other electricity is converted from natural power, such as water, wind, and Sun. Nuclear energy also provides a source of electricity. However, the constant demand strains our resources. New alternatives need to be found. We also need to save, or conserve, electricity. The list below identifies ways you and your family can conserve electricity.

Check the correct boxes to answer the questions.

	Yes	No
1. Do you turn off the light when you are the last person to leave the room?	☐	☐
2. Are all of the bulbs used in your home the proper brightness for their use?	☐	☐
3. Do you make sure that all the small appliances in your home are used only when necessary?	☐	☐
4. Do you make sure the television, radio, or record player are turned off when no one is watching or listening?	☐	☐
5. Do you use the clothes washer and dryer only when they have a full load?	☐	☐
6. Do you use your large appliances only at off-peak usage hours?	☐	☐
7. Have you tried to use appliances that were designed to save energy?	☐	☐
8. Do you set the air conditioner so that it runs at top efficiency?	☐	☐
9. Do you use the dishwasher only when it has a full load?	☐	☐
10. Do you follow your monthly use of electricity to see if you are conserving?	☐	☐

Name _____   Date _____

Electric Safety

You are learning about the uses of electricity. In this activity you will see how safe your home is electrically.

SAFETY TIP: THIS ACTIVITY MUST BE SUPERVISED BY AN ADULT.

Check the answer to each question below.

		Yes	No
1.	Do all outlets have only the proper number of plugs in them?	☐	☐
2.	Are all of these plugs in safe condition? (no breaks or cracks)	☐	☐
3.	Are all cords placed where they are safe, where no one can walk or trip on them?	☐	☐
4.	Are all cords in safe condition? (no breaks or cracks)	☐	☐
5.	Do all appliances plug directly into an outlet without extension cords?	☐	☐
6.	Are large appliances with three-pronged plugs properly grounded?	☐	☐
7.	Is each large appliance plugged into its own circuit?	☐	☐
8.	Can you find the electrical service panel for your home?	☐	☐
9.	Does each fuse or circuit breaker show which circuits it controls?	☐	☐
10.	Could you turn off all of the electricity in an emergency?	☐	☐

If you have answered *no* to any of the questions above, you probably have some safety problems that should be corrected. You may be able to correct some problems yourself. If you cannot, you should contact an electrician or the electric company.

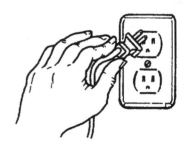

Unit 1: A Charge for Life

Safety First

What would we do without electricity? We'd spend a lot of time in the dark without electric lights. There would be no TV, no movies, no computers. It's hard to imagine a modern world without the benefits of electricity. As useful as electricity is, it also has dangers. The amount of electricity that flows through the wiring in your home is enough to kill you. But used wisely, electricity is very safe.

One of the first things you may have learned as a toddler was to stay away from electric outlets. Making contact with the wiring inside the outlet is very dangerous. Even though the wiring is inside the outlet, electricity can jump across the small gap to your hand. But materials such as plastic insulate, or block, the path of the electricity. For this reason, the plugs on electric cords are made of plastic. When you hold the plastic plug, your hand is protected from the flow of electricity. You should always hold onto only the plastic part of the plug. Never touch the metal prongs when you are plugging something into a socket.

Outlet protectors are also made of plastic. These small, flat plugs fit into an outlet and protect small children and pets from accidentally making contact with the flow of electricity.

Electric cords are made of wires that are coated with plastic. The electricity travels along the wires, and the plastic insulates the wires. When a cord gets old, the plastic can break. When this happens, the wires can touch each other and cause a dangerous shock or start a fire. Many home fires are started by problems in electric wiring. Never use an electric appliance that has a broken or worn cord.

Unlike plastic, some materials are not insulators but are conductors. Water, for example, is a very good conductor of electricity. For this reason, you need to be very careful about using electricity near water. For example, never touch an electric appliance with wet hands. Do not turn the dial on a radio or plug a cord into an outlet when your hands are wet. The water could conduct the electricity to your hands.

Be especially careful using electric appliances in the kitchen or bathroom. For example, never use a hair dryer or any other electric appliance while you are in the bathtub.

You also need to be aware of electricity in nature. Lightning, which is a form of static electricity, can be very dangerous. If at all possible, do not go outdoors during an

GO ON TO THE NEXT PAGE

Safety First, p. 2

electrical storm. Lightning tends to strike the tallest thing in an area. For example, if there is one tree in an open field, lightning would most likely hit the tree before it hit anything else. For this reason, never stand under a tree during an electrical storm.

Many electrical storms occur during warm weather, which is when people go swimming. If lightning strikes a pool or pond, the electricity will flow throughout the whole body of water, and anything in the water will get shocked. Never swim during an electrical storm. Get out of the water the first time you hear thunder, and do not get back into the water for at least 15 minutes after the last time you hear thunder.

Answer the questions.

1. Sometimes the air gets very hot and still right before it starts to rain. Why might this not be a good time to go swimming?

   _____

   _____

2. Why do you have to be careful about the way you hold a plug when you plug an electric appliance into a socket?

   _____

   _____

3. Why do you have to be especially careful using electric appliances in the kitchen and bathroom?

   _____

   _____

4. Why is it sometimes unsafe to try to stay dry under a tree?

   _____

   _____

Unit 1: A Charge for Life

Unit 1 Science Fair Ideas

A science fair project can help you to understand the world around you. Choose a topic that interests you. Then use the scientific method to develop your project. Here's an example:

1. **Problem:** What part of a magnet has the most force?

2. **Hypothesis:** The poles of a magnet have more magnetic force.

3. **Experimentation:** Materials: different shaped magnets, paper clips, centimeter ruler.
   - Find out how many paper clips each pole of the magnets will hold.
   - Find out how many paper clips the center of each magnet will hold.
   - Measure the strength of each magnet. Place a paper clip at one end of the ruler and the end of a magnet at the other. Slowly slide the magnet closer to the clip. When the paper clip starts to move, read the distance it is from the magnet.
   - Repeat the above step using the center of the magnets.

4. **Observation:** The poles of the magnets attracted the most paper clips. The end of the magnet was also a greater distance from the paper clip before it moved.

5. **Conclusion:** The poles of the magnet have the greatest magnetic force.

6. **Comparison:** The conclusion and the hypothesis agree.

7. **Presentation:** Prepare a presentation or a report to explain your results. If possible, set up the materials so that other people can try the experiment.

8. **Resources:** Tell the books you used to find background information. Tell who helped you to get the materials and set up the experiment.

Other Project Ideas

1. Computers use electrical circuits on silicon chips. Research to find out what kind of circuits are used and how they work.
2. How do people use wind to make energy? Do research on windmills and plan a project.
3. How are a lemon and a dry cell the same? Find out which foods produce electric energy.

Unit 2 Keep on Moving!

INTRODUCTION

Every day, students observe a variety of actions, reactions, and machines that utilize the basic concepts of force and motion. By fifth grade, students can better understand the underlying principles of force, gravity, friction, and inertia. Moreover, they will explore in closer detail Newton's laws of motion.

FORCE

A force is simply a push or a pull and always happens in pairs. Forces can be balanced or unbalanced, and it is the interactions of these kinds of forces that create motion. If forces are balanced, there is no movement. For example, if a kite is not moving while you are flying it, the force of the wind is balancing the weight of the kite and the pull of the string. However, if the wind stops blowing, the weight of the kite and the pull of the string would be greater, causing the forces to become unbalanced. The kite would then move.

Forces also differ in size and direction. To move a book, it takes a small amount of force; but to move a bookshelf, it would take much more force. Forces can also come from up, down, left, and right. A force can be measured. Sometimes it is hard for students to understand that when pushing or pulling an object, even though the object does not move, the push or pull can be measured.

Force is measured in newtons. They can be added and subtracted. If forces are going in the same direction, they are added. For example, if someone is pushing a wagon and another person is pulling a wagon, the amount of forces being exerted can be added together. However, if people are pulling in opposite directions, say in a tug-of-war, the forces would be subtracted. The team having the greater number of newtons would have a greater force and would win.

Inertia

Inertia is the tendency for all objects to stay still or to keep moving if they are moving. There is only a change in the speed or direction when an outside force acts on the object. This concept is known as the *first law of motion,* or the *first law of inertia,* and was explained by Sir Isaac Newton in the 1700s.

Inertia is a property of mass. The more mass an object has, the more it resists a change in its state. Likewise, the greater the mass, the greater the inertia. Once an object is moving, it tends to maintain its direction and speed. It will continue to move in a straight line unless acted upon by another, unbalanced force. A person riding in a car travels at the same speed as the car. The person has the same rate of inertia. But if the car stops, the person's inertia tendency is continued at the same speed and direction. The seatbelt acts as an outside force to stop the forward movement.

Gravity

Gravity is a force that attracts all objects that have mass. It is the force that keeps all objects from flying off the surface of the Earth. It is also the force that keeps the planets, Moon, and stars in orbit. Everything on Earth is pulled to the center of the Earth by this unseen force. Sir Isaac Newton called this force *gravitation;* and he explained that all things had force, but that the pull of the Earth was greater, thus anchoring objects to the Earth's surface and making things fall down. The more massive an object, the greater the force that will be exerted. The force of gravitation is about 9.8 newtons per kilometer for every object on Earth.

Gravitational force depends on the mass of an object and how far apart the centers of the objects are. The more mass an object has, the greater the gravitational pull will be. The gravitational force between the Earth and other objects is greater because the mass of the Earth is so large. If the mass of two objects is small, the gravitational force will also be small because the force of the Earth's gravity is greater. For example, if two books are side by side on a table, they will stay on the table because of the pull of gravity from Earth. If the forces of gravity and friction were not working, the books would move toward each other. Furthermore, the farther apart the bodies are, the less the pull will be because less force can be exerted.

Another concept difficult for students to understand is the difference in the terms *mass* and *weight.* Mass is the measure of the amount of matter in an object. As discussed in Unit 1, mass is measured in grams (g). Weight is the measure of the force of gravity on an object. A spring scale measures weight using newtons. When students step on a scale, they are actually measuring their mass, since weight is measured in newtons. It can best be explained by comparing the mass and weight of a person on Earth and on the Moon. The mass of the person stays the same in either place. However, the weight of the person on the Moon will be one sixth of the weight on Earth. The gravitational pull is one sixth less on the Moon since the Moon has less mass.

Friction

Friction is a force that keeps resting objects from moving and tends to slow motion when one object rubs against another object. Every motion is affected by friction. It is useful when movement needs to be slowed, but it causes problems when something needs to be moved. An object's surface determines the amount of friction. Rough surfaces, like concrete, dirt, and grass, create more friction. This is helpful when walking, so that people can walk without sliding. These surfaces create a problem when trying to move something over them. Smooth surfaces, like ice and lacquered wood, have less friction, so motion would be easier. Moreover, heat is produced as the objects rub across each other. Early humans used the force of friction to make fire when they rubbed two sticks together.

Mass and surface areas of objects affect the amount of friction. The heavier an object is, the greater the amount of friction. By lightening the load, friction will be decreased, and the load can be moved more easily with less force. Similarly, when large surface areas come into contact during motion, friction is greater. By reducing the contact of the surface areas, the object can be moved more easily.

There are three kinds of friction: fluid, rolling, and sliding. Fluid friction is the friction created when an object comes into contact with water or gas, such as an airplane flying through the air. Rolling friction is the force produced by balls or wheels coming into contact with another surface, such as the wheels of a car on a road. Sliding friction occurs when objects slide across each other, such as the action of pushing a box across the floor.

In some cases, friction can be reduced by using lubricants, materials like oil or soap. Lubricants coat the surface of an object to decrease rubbing. Machines need lubricants to reduce the friction when parts rub against each other. This helps to keep the parts cool to avoid fire hazards as well as to keep them moving smoothly.

Action and Reaction

Newton's third law of motion states that for every action, there is an equal and opposite reaction. When an object pushes or pulls in one direction, the action, there is another push or pull in the opposite direction, the reaction. For example, when a bat hits a baseball, the ball reacts by moving in the opposite direction. If the forces are equal, or balanced, there is no motion. This is exemplified by a book lying on a table. The book is being pulled by the force of gravity, but the table is reacting by pushing up. The result is that the book remains at rest.

Motion

Motion is the movement of an object. We can tell if an object moves by comparing it to something that does not move, a frame of reference. Most motion is compared to the Sun, Moon, stars, or other objects that are far away and appear not to move. You can determine how fast or slow an object moves by measuring its speed. Speed is the distance an object moves in a given amount of time. To calculate speed, use this formula:

$$\text{Speed} = \frac{\text{Distance traveled}}{\text{Time traveled}}$$

Velocity describes the direction of an object. Velocity is the speed of an object in a given direction. It includes both speed and direction. If either speed or direction changes, then velocity changes, too. Motion can also be affected by gravity, outside forces of cables or strings, or a collision between objects. A collision can start or stop a motion, or change the direction of a motion.

Acceleration

Any change in the speed or direction of an object is acceleration. Newton's second law of motion states that an object accelerates faster as the force gets larger or the object's mass gets smaller. In other words, it takes less force to move an object with a smaller amount of mass. Moreover, if a force pushes or pulls an object in the same direction, there is positive acceleration. Negative acceleration occurs when a force pushes or pulls an object in the opposite direction than it is moving.

Energy

Energy is the ability to cause change. Potential energy is the energy stored in an object because of its position. Objects that bend, stretch, or compress, like a rubber band, have elastic potential energy. Those objects that have the ability to fall, like a roller-coaster car on the brink of a hill, have gravitational potential energy. Potential energy can be converted to kinetic energy, the energy of a moving object. The same roller-coaster car that has gravitational potential energy changes its energy to kinetic energy as soon as it begins to descend.

Name _____   Date _____

How Does It Move?

The physical world is constantly in motion. Each time you describe something that is moving, you are comparing it with another object or a background that you assume is not moving. This background or object is your frame of reference. The most basic frame of reference we use is the movement of the Earth around the Sun. Even ancient people observed the Earth's relationship to the Sun and the stars. They built structures, such as Casa Grande in Arizona, to observe the apparent movement of the Sun and the stars.

 Complete the sentences.

1. Comparing the motion of an object with a background that is not moving is using a _____.

2. When you change your frame of reference, your perception of _____ changes, too.

 Answer the question.

3. Give an example of a frame of reference you have experienced.

_____

_____

_____

_____

_____

_____

_____

Unit 2: Keep on Moving!

Name _____ Date _____

Where Is the Frame of Reference?

When you describe movement, you are comparing it to something that you think is not moving. This nonmoving object or background is the frame of reference.

 You will need:
pencil

1. Hold the pencil out front at arm's length. Close one eye.

2. Move your head and the pencil to the left and then to the right. What appears to move?

3. Now, move your head left and right, but hold the pencil still. What appears to move?

 _____
Answer the questions.

1. In Step 2, what appears to be moving?

_____

2. What is the frame of reference?

_____

3. In Step 3, what appears to be moving?

_____

4. What is the frame of reference?

_____

Name _____   Date _____

Measuring Speed

Speed is the distance an object moves in a certain amount of time. To find speed, use this formula: $\text{Speed} = \dfrac{\text{distance traveled}}{\text{time traveled}}$

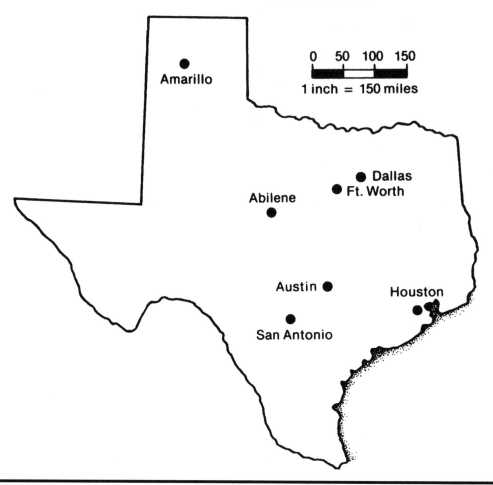

Use the map scale to find the distances between the cities. Round to the nearest whole number.

1. If you travel at an average speed of 50 mph, how long will it take to drive from Dallas to Houston? _____ Houston to San Antonio? _____ San Antonio to Austin? _____

2. What would be your average speed if it takes

   5 hr from Amarillo to Abilene? _____

   2 hr 45 min from Abilene to Dallas? _____

   4 hr 30 min from Fort Worth to Austin? _____

Unit 2: Keep on Moving!

Physical Science 5, SV 3764-X

How Do You Measure the Speed of a Marble?

Speed is the distance an object moves in a certain amount of time. To find speed, use this formula: $\text{Speed} = \dfrac{\text{distance traveled}}{\text{time traveled}}$

✔ **You will need:**

book	ruler with pencil groove
meter stick	masking tape
glass marble	clock with second hand

1. Work with a partner. Put the book on the floor. Place the end of the ruler on the edge of the book to make a ramp.

2. Measure 5 m from one edge of the book across the floor. Mark the point with a piece of tape.

3. Have your partner look at the second hand of the clock. When your partner says "Go," let the marble go from the top of the ramp.

4. As the marble rolls toward the tape, your partner should count the seconds that go by. When the marble reaches the tape, you should say, "Stop."

5. Record the distance and the time in the table on page 64. Use the formula to find the speed of the marble. Record the speed on the table.

6. Repeat Steps 3-5 for three more trials.

GO ON TO THE NEXT PAGE ➤

How Do You Measure the Speed of a Marble?, p. 2

Marble Speed

Trial	Distance	Time (sec)	Speed (m/sec)
1			
2			
3			
4			

Answer the questions.

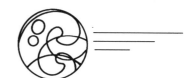

1. Was the speed the same for each trial?

   _____

   _____

2. If the speeds were different, find the average speed by adding the speeds and dividing by 4.

   _____

   _____

3. Explain why an average speed should be found.

   _____

   _____

4. What factor caused the speed of the rolling marble to change from one trial to the next?

   _____

   _____

Unit 2: Keep on Moving!
Physical Science 5, SV 3764-X

Name _____   Date _____

Velocity

You are probably familiar with the formula *Speed = distance ÷ time*. You use this formula to find how fast an object such as a car is moving. If the length of the sidewalk in front of your school is 61 meters (200 feet), and you can ride your bike the length of the walk in 18 seconds, then your speed is 61 meters divided by 18 seconds, or 3.4 meters per second (11 feet per second).

Velocity is a term that refers to both speed and direction. If you are going east when you ride in front of the school, then your velocity is 3.4 meters per second east. You could also express the velocity as 12.2 kilometers per hour east, abbreviated as 12.2 km/hr east (7.6 miles per hour east, 7.6 mi/hr east).

An object traveling parallel to another has, in addition to its own velocity, a velocity relative to the object traveling with it. For example, suppose that one car passes another on a highway. The first car has a velocity of 80 km/hr (50 mi/hr) east. The second car has a velocity of 97 km/hr (60 mi/hr) east. How fast is the second car going relative to the first car? To find out, subtract the first velocity from the second: 97 − 80 = 17 km/hr east. In other words, the second car is pulling ahead of the first one at the rate of 17 km/hr east. Knowing this, you can calculate how much earlier the second car will arrive at a certain point.

Objects traveling in opposite directions also have velocities relative to each other. Suppose a train left New York and was traveling at a rate of 129 km/hr (80 mi/hr) west. At the same time, a train left Chicago and was traveling east at a rate of 112 km/hr (70 mi/hr) east. To find how fast they were traveling relative to each other, or how fast the gap between them was closing, add the two velocities. The gap between these two trains was closing at a rate of 129 + 112 = 241 km/hr (150 mi/hr).

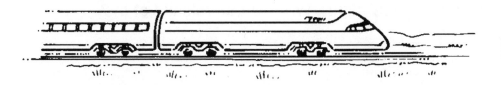

GO ON TO THE NEXT PAGE

Velocity, p. 2

Answer the questions.

1. John and Tom live near each other and work at the same job. John leaves for work at 7 A.M. and drives at a velocity of 48 km/hr (30 mi/hr) east. Tom leaves 15 minutes later and drives at a velocity of 64 km/hr (40 mi/hr) east. What is Tom's velocity relative to John's?

   _____

2. Why do we subtract when calculating relative velocities of vehicles traveling in the same direction? _____

   _____

   _____

   _____

3. In what way could it be useful to know the relative velocities of vehicles traveling in parallel? _____

   _____

   _____

   _____

4. Mary and Yolanda live at opposite ends of town, and they recently decided to meet for lunch. They left their homes at the same time. Mary was traveling at a velocity of 56 km/hr (35 mi/hr) east. Yolanda had to go through town, where there is a speed limit of 40 km/hr (25 mi/hr). How fast was the gap closing between them? _____

5. An airplane leaves New York bound for California. Its airspeed is 1,030 km/hr (640 mi/hr). At the same time, an airplane leaves California bound for New York. They are heading toward each other (at different altitudes) at a speed of 2,042 km/hr (1,269 mi/hr). What is the velocity of the eastbound airplane? _____

Objects at Rest

Objects at rest tend to stay at rest. You can show that this statement is true by doing the following tests.

A.  **You will need:**
paper towel   cup   pebbles

1. Fill the cup nearly full with pebbles. Spread the paper towel out on a table. Place the cup on the towel near one corner.

2. Pick up the opposite corner of the towel. Quickly pull the towel away. What happens?

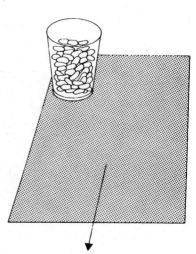

_____

_____

_____

B. **You will need:**
paper   paper clip   clear plastic cup

1. Make a straight line down the center of the paper with a pencil. Turn the cup on its side. Place it on top of the pencil line as shown.

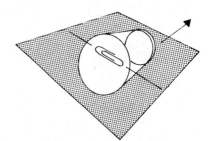

2. Put the paper clip inside the cup. Line it up with the pencil mark.

3. Hold the bottom of the cup in one hand. Quickly pull it to the right. What happens?

_____

_____

_____

_____

Unit 2: Keep on Moving!

Inertia

All things have inertia. Read these three facts about inertia.

A. An object at rest tends to stay at rest.

B. Once in motion, an object remains in motion in a straight line.

C. A moving object continues to move in a straight line unless acted upon by an outside force.

Look at the pictures below and read about each one. Decide which of the above facts best describes each picture. Write the letter of this fact on the line below each picture.

1.

_____

When a moving car stops suddenly, the people in it keep moving.

2.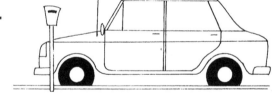

_____

Gravitation pulls on the Moon. This causes it to revolve around Earth in a circular path.

3.

_____

The ball is not moving.

4.

_____

The car remains in one place.

5.

_____

The child moves down the slide.

6.

_____

The satellite orbits Earth.

Unit 2: Keep on Moving!

Name _____   Date _____

How Can You Compare the Inertia of Two Objects?

The amount of matter in an object is its mass. More mass in an object also means that it has more inertia. More force will be needed to move it, because it has a greater tendency to remain at rest.

 You will need:
steel washer, 4–5 cm in diameter
30 cm metal strip   rubber band   3 books
clock with second hand   rock, 2–4 cm in diameter

1. Work with a partner. Use the rubber band to attach the washer to the metal strip.

2. Stack the three books on the edge of a table.

3. Place 10 cm of the strip underneath the books.

4. Push the washer end of the strip down about 5 cm. Have your partner look at the second hand of the clock. When your partner says "Go," let the strip go.

5. The strip moves quickly up and down. Each time it moves down, it makes one vibration. Have your partner time 10 seconds. Count the number of vibrations. When your partner says "Stop," record the number of vibrations on the table on page 70.

6. Repeat Steps 4 and 5 two more times.

7. Find the average number of vibrations of the three trials.

8. Now attach the small rock to the end of the strip. Repeat Steps 3–7.

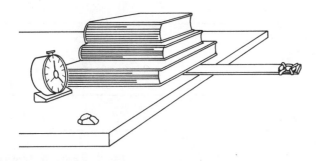

GO ON TO THE NEXT PAGE ➡

How Can You Compare the Inertia of Two Objects?, p. 2

Inertia Comparison

Metal Strip with Washer	Vibrations per 10 Seconds	Metal Strip with Rock	Vibrations per 10 Seconds
Trial 1		Trial 1	
Trial 2		Trial 2	
Trial 3		Trial 3	
Total		Total	
Average		Average	

Answer the questions.

1. What was the average number of vibrations for the strip with the washer?

   _____

   _____

2. What was the average number of vibrations for the strip with the rock?

   _____

   _____

3. Was it easier for the strip to move the washer or the rock? Why?

   _____

   _____

4. Which object had greater inertia? Why?

   _____

   _____

5. Which object had greater mass? Why?

   _____

   _____

Accelerometer

The rate of change in velocity, or change in velocity over time, is called *acceleration.* Whether an object is speeding up, slowing down, or changing direction, it is accelerating. When an object slows down, or the velocity decreases, we sometimes say the object is decelerating. However, in scientific language, any change in velocity is called acceleration.

 You will need:

clear plastic bottle with cap   water   small piece of bar soap

1. Fill the bottle with water, leaving enough space for a small air bubble. Add the piece of bar soap so that the bubble will not attach to the wall of the bottle.

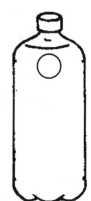

2. Screw the cap on the bottle. Set the bottle on its side on a table. The bubble should move to the center of the side that is up.

3. Pick up the bottle. Quickly push the bottle forward. What happened to the bubble?

4. Pull the bottle quickly back toward you. What happened to the bubble?

5. Carry the bottle as you walk in a straight path, then turn left and continue to walk in a straight path. What happened to the bubble?

Answer the questions.

1. What kinds of movement made the bubble move?

_____

_____

2. How are velocity and acceleration related?

_____

_____

Acceleration

A force is a push or pull. When a force pushes or pulls an object in the opposite direction, there is negative acceleration. If it moves in the same direction, there is positive acceleration.

Study these 4 pictures.

a. Identify the force acting on the object in each picture.

b. Determine whether the object is undergoing positive acceleration or negative acceleration.

1.

a. _____

b. _____

2.

a. _____

b. _____

3.

a. _____

b. _____

4.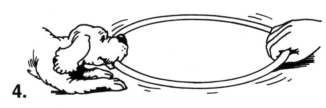

a. _____

b. _____

Unit 2: Keep on Moving!

How Does Mass Affect Acceleration?

Newton's second law of motion states that an object accelerates faster as the force gets larger or as the mass of the object gets smaller.

> ## ✔ You will need:
>
> | | | |
> |---|---|---|
> | 3 Styrofoam cups | pin | masking tape |
> | toy truck | sand | string |
> | pennies | water | ruler   scissors |

1. Label the cups *A, B,* and *C.*

2. Punch a hole in the bottom of cup C using the pin. Make a pencil mark 1.5 cm up from the bottom of the cup on the inside. Tape the cup to the back of the toy truck.

3. Fill cup B with sand. Put the cup in the back of the truck.

4. Place the truck at one end of a table. Tie one end of the string to the front of the truck. Tie the other end through cup A.

5. Extend the string the length of the table. Let the string and cup A drop 30 cm over the edge of the table.

6. Drop some pennies into cup A until it moves.

7. Move the truck back to the starting point. Fill cup C with water up to the pencil mark. Let the truck go. Measure the distance between the drops of water that fall to the table from the hole in the bottom of the cup. Record it on the table on page 74.

8. Remove the sand-filled cup B from the truck. Repeat Steps 6 and 7.

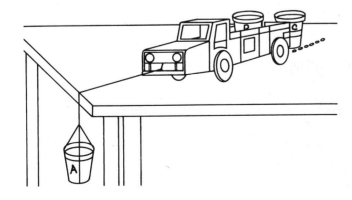

GO ON TO THE NEXT PAGE ➤

Unit 2: Keep on Moving!

How Does Mass Affect Acceleration?, p. 2

Measuring Acceleration

Truck	Distance Between Drops
With Sand	
Without Sand	

 Answer the questions.

1. What part of the experiment is the force?

   _____

2. What was the distance between the drops of water that fell from the truck carrying sand?

   _____

3. What was the distance between the drops of water that fell from the truck without sand?

   _____

4. Which way did the truck accelerate faster, with the sand or without the sand? How do you know?

   _____

5. What caused the difference in acceleration?

   _____

   _____

Name _____   Date _____

Understanding Acceleration

Did you ever ride a roller coaster? Look at the picture of the roller coaster on this page. Note the location of the letters **A**, **B**, **C**, and **D** on the picture. Read the sentences that describe what is happening at the places marked with the letters. Then write the correct letter on the line beside each sentence. You may use a letter more than once, and some answers may have more than one letter.

1. _____ The cars have the lowest velocity.

2. _____ The cars have the highest velocity.

3. _____ The cars are gaining speed.

4. _____ The cars are losing speed.

5. _____ There is positive acceleration.

6. _____ There is negative acceleration.

7. _____ There is no acceleration.

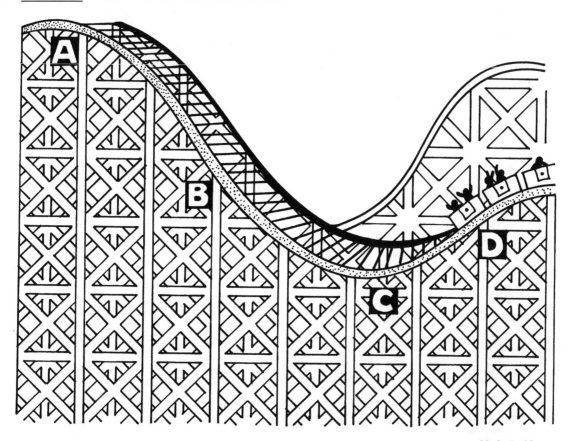

Kinds of Energy

Motion involves energy. Energy is the ability to cause change. At the top of a hill, a roller coaster has *potential energy*—the energy stored in an object. As the roller coaster descends, its potential energy is converted to *kinetic energy*, the energy of movement. The energy stored in an object that can bend or stretch and then return to its original shape is called *elastic potential energy*. This energy can be observed in items such as a rubber band or a stretched spring. The energy an object has because of its ability to fall is *gravitational potential energy*. A marble held above the floor has this kind of potential energy. When you drop the marble, the gravitational potential energy is converted into kinetic energy. The higher you hold the marble, the greater the energy it has.

An object in motion has *momentum*. An object's momentum is its mass multiplied by its velocity. If its mass or velocity is large, an object will have a large momentum. The more momentum an object has, the harder it is to stop the object or to change its direction.

Underline the best answer.

1. A diver poised on a diving board has . . .
   a. kinetic energy.
   b. mechanical energy.
   c. gravitational potential energy.
   d. elastic potential energy.
2. As the diver jumps, the board bends down. At this point the board has . . .
   a. kinetic energy.
   b. mechanical energy.
   c. gravitational potential energy.
   d. elastic potential energy.
3. As the diver plunges into the water, the diver has . . .
   a. kinetic energy.
   b. mechanical energy.
   c. gravitational potential energy.
   d. elastic potential energy.

4. Which has the greatest momentum?
   a. a bowling ball traveling at 10 kilometers per hour (kph)
   b. a bowling ball traveling at 20 kph
   c. a basketball traveling at 10 kph
   d. a basketball traveling at 20 kph
5. Describe the changes in energy that take place when children hit a piñata, the piñata breaks, and the candy and toys fall out.

_____

_____

How Does a Carousel Work?

Kinetic energy is the mechanical energy of a moving object. If something has mass movement, it has kinetic energy. Potential energy is the stored energy of an object that is the result of its position.

You will need:

plastic liter bottle	plastic dish detergent bottle
long, thin rubber band	2 thin wooden dowels
cap paper clip	tape wire
bead 4 paper cups	string scissors

1. Ask your teacher to punch a hole in the bottom of the bottle and to remove the nozzle of the cap.

2. Loop one end of the rubber band over a paper clip. Thread the other end of the rubber band through the bottom of the bottle.

3. Make a hook on one end of the wire. Catch the free end of the rubber band inside the bottle and pull it out through the opening. Thread the wire through the opening in the cap, pulling the wire and rubber band all the way out. Slip the bead over the end of the wire. Tighten the cap on the bottle.

4. Cross the wooden dowels and tape them together at right angles. Attach the cross to the bottle by winding the free end of the wire around the cross.

5. Tape strings to the bottom of each cup. Tape the other end to the end of the dowels.

6. Turn the cross to wind the rubber band. Let it go. Watch what happens.

Unit 2: Keep on Moving!

How Does a Carousel Work?, p. 2

Answer the questions.

1. When does your carousel have the greatest potential energy?

_____

_____

2. What gives it potential energy?

_____

_____

3. When is the potential energy converted to kinetic energy?

_____

_____

4. How is the movement of the carousel related to the rubber band?

_____

_____

_____

Coin Crashes

Baseballs and some plastic balls are the same size and shape. They can be thrown at about the same speed. So why does catching a baseball feel different from catching a plastic ball? The difference is caused by a difference in the momentums of the balls. You can think of momentum as a measure of the ball's force.

Each ball's momentum depends on two things: its mass and its speed. You can calculate the amount of momentum of each ball by multiplying its mass by its speed.

How do the momentums of a baseball and a plastic ball compare when both balls are moving at the same speed? The momentum of the baseball is greater than the momentum of the plastic ball because the baseball has more mass. The greater momentum of the moving baseball gives it more of a wallop when you catch it. The baseball's greater momentum also makes the baseball more likely to break a window if it hits one.

✔ **You will need:**

large sheet of cardboard		metric ruler
pencil	3 pennies	masking tape
1 nickel	1 quarter	

1. Lay the cardboard on a smooth tabletop. Near the center of the cardboard, use the metric ruler to draw a straight line across it. Label the line *1*. At a distance of 2 cm to the right of line 1, draw another straight line, parallel to line 1. Label the line *2*. At 20 cm to the right of line 2, draw a third straight line, parallel to line 2. Label the line *3*.

2. Place two pennies about 10 cm apart on line 1. Use small pieces of masking tape to label the pennies *A* and *B*.

GO ON TO THE NEXT PAGE ➤

Unit 2: Keep on Moving!

Coin Crashes, p. 2

3. Line up the third penny on line 3 directly behind penny A. Line up the nickel on line 3 directly behind penny B.

4. Use the ruler to slide the penny quickly from line 3 to line 2. Be sure that you don't push the ruler beyond line 2. Try to slide the penny so that it hits penny A straight on. Measure the distance penny A moves. Record this distance under *Trial 1* for penny A in the table.

5. Use the ruler to slide the nickel quickly from line 3 to line 2. Be sure that you don't push the ruler beyond line 2. Try to slide the nickel at the same speed you slid the penny. Slide the nickel so that it hits penny B straight on. Measure the distance penny B moves. Record this distance under *Trial 1* for penny B in the table.

6. Replace pennies A and B along line 1. Replace the penny and the nickel along line 3. Repeat steps 4 and 5 for Trials 2–5. For each trial, try to slide the penny and the nickel at the same speed as you did in Trial 1. Record the results in the table.

Distance Penny Moved (cm)

Penny	Trial 1	Trial 2	Trial 3	Trial 4	Trial 5
A					
B					

Answer the questions.

1. Look at the table. Did the penny or the nickel cause the pennies to move farther?

_____

2. Did the penny or the nickel—traveling at the same speed—have the greater momentum? Explain.

_____

The Direction of Force

A force is a push or a pull. Forces have magnitude and direction. A force can start an object moving, change the direction and rate of its motion, or change the shape of the object. Any force acts in a specific direction with a specific size or strength. Forces can be combined to increase their effect. You can illustrate a force by using an arrow. The head of the arrow shows the direction of the force. The tail of the arrow identifies the point where the force is exerted.

Look at the pictures.

1. Draw arrows to indicate the direction and strength of the forces.

   a.

   b.

2. Identify the following activities as pushes or pulls. Write *push* or *pull* on the line in front of the statement.

   a. _____ hitting a tennis ball   **b.** _____ painting a wall

   c. _____ brushing your teeth   **d.** _____ brushing your hair

   e. _____ writing with a pencil   **f.** _____ rowing a boat

   g. _____ pedaling a bicycle   **h.** _____ climbing a rope

Exercising Force

What do you think of when you hear the word *work*? Do you think about playing on the playground? Probably not. Yet, when you use playground or exercise equipment, you are doing work. You do work when you use force to move an object.

The muscles of your body act in pairs to help you do work. One muscle contracts, or gets shorter, while another muscle relaxes. The pair of muscles acts together to exert a force.

When you walk across a room, you are doing work. You are exerting force to move an object, your body, across some distance. The muscles in your legs produce a pushing force on the ground. It is this force that causes your body to move.

Answer the questions.

1. In the drawing, what exercise equipment is the boy using and what work is he doing?

   _____

   _____

2. What groups of muscles are used on this piece of equipment?

   _____

   _____

3. In what direction is he applying the force on the equipment?

   _____

   _____

4. When you kick a soccer ball, what muscles do you use and in what direction do you apply a force?

   _____

   _____

Can You Observe the Direction of Opposite Forces?

Forces always occur together. When there is one force, whether an object is still or moving, there is another force working in the opposition direction—a reaction. Newton's third law of motion states that for every action, there is an equal and opposite reaction.

✔ **You will need:**

scissors	1 qt milk carton
balloon	tape
sink or tub filled with water 5 cm deep	

1. Cut the milk carton in half lengthwise. Cut a small notch in the bottom of the milk carton.

2. Blow up the balloon, but do not tie it.

3. While holding the air of the balloon in, tape the balloon in the milk carton. Place the end you are holding into the notch.

4. Put the carton in a tub of water.

5. Release the balloon so the air flows out of the balloon.

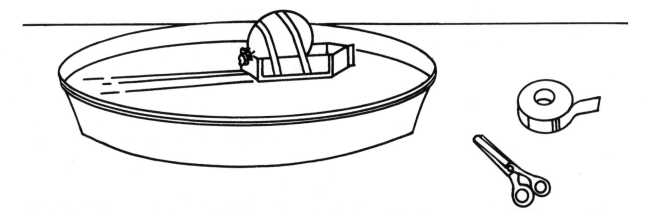

GO ON TO THE NEXT PAGE

Unit 2: Keep on Moving!

Can You Observe the Direction of Opposite Forces?, p. 2

Answer the questions.

1. Which way did the air coming out of the balloon move?

_____

_____

2. Which way did the carton move?

_____

_____

3. Which force was the action force?

_____

_____

4. Which force was the reaction force?

_____

_____

5. What scientific law did you observe in this activity?

_____

_____

6. How is the force of the air in the balloon like a propeller in a boat?

_____

_____

_____

_____

Unit 2: Keep on Moving!

Opposite Forces

Forces always happen in pairs. Newton's third law of motion states that for every action, there is an equal and opposite reaction. When an object pushes or pulls in one direction, there is another push or pull in the opposite direction—a reaction.

A. In the spaces provided, draw pictures that show the action and reaction forces for:
1. a book resting on a desk.
2. a parachute opened in air.
3. a ball being kicked.
4. a rocket being launched.

B. Label the forces, and use arrows to show their direction.

1.	2.
3.	**4.**

Building Science Vocabulary

Fill in the blanks with the correct words from the Word List. You may use a word more than once.

Word List
inertia
time
reference point
distance
force
mass
accelerated
velocity
speed

The oil supertanker passed the coastline on the way into the harbor.
As it passed, the navigation officer took a second bearing on his
1. _____, the lighthouse on the coast. Then he
divided the **2.** _____ the ship had traveled since his first observation
by the **3.** _____ between his two observations. He found that the
ship's **4.** _____ or **5.** _____ was 6 nautical miles per hour
(knots). Turning to the captain he reported, "We're making 6 knots, sir. Time
to reduce speed."

The captain knew that the vessel needed a huge **6.** _____ to slow
it, or to accelerate its huge **7.** _____. So he called for the engines
to reduce to "Slow Ahead." To slow down the ship, he made use of the
8. _____ of the water as it is parted by the curving bow of the ship.

Forty minutes later the captain signaled for all engines to stop. But because
of its **9.** _____, the vessel kept moving straight ahead. Gradually,
the huge and constant **10.** _____ of water slowed the ship. At last
the captain called for "Full Astern." The mighty force of the propellers
11. _____ the ship to a dead stop. The engines were
shut down. Lines were made fast to the anchor buoy. Another voyage was
entered in the log.

Unit 2: Keep on Moving!

The Force of Gravity

Gravity is the force that pulls objects in the universe toward one another. Earth is surrounded by a gravitational field that decreases in strength as the distance from Earth increases. The size of the force of gravity between any two objects is determined by the masses of the objects and the distance between them. Mass is the amount of matter.

✔ **You will need:**

golf ball	large marble
Ping-Pong ball	rubber ball (from jacks)
ruler	small wooden ball

1. Work with a partner. Choose three balls.

2. Place all three balls on the edge of the table about 4 cm apart. Predict which ball will hit the ground first, when all are pushed off the table at the same time.

3. Hold the ruler so that the side with numbers faces the balls. Gently push the balls off the table at the same time. Your partner should look at the floor to see which ball hits the floor first.

4. Record your observation on page 88 on the table under *Trial 1*.

5. Repeat Steps 2 and 3 two more times. Record your observations on the table.

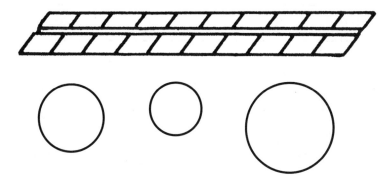

GO ON TO THE NEXT PAGE ▶

Unit 2: Keep on Moving!

The Force of Gravity, p. 2

Ball Drop

Trial	Observation
Trial 1	
Trial 2	
Trial 3	

Answer the questions.

1. What did you observe about the order in which the balls hit the ground?

_____

_____

2. How is the force of gravity acting on the balls related to their mass?

_____

_____

_____

3. How is gravity a force?

_____

_____

_____

Name _____ Date _____

How Much Force?

A newton is the unit used to measure force. One newton (N) is equal to the force of Earth's gravity on a 100-gram (g) mass. This means that if you are on Earth and you want to lift a 100-gram mass, you would have to exert a force of 1 newton.

The table below shows how much force would be required to lift various objects on Earth as well as on two other planets, called planet X and planet Y. Study the table, and then answer the questions that follow.

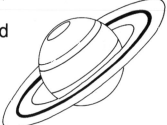

Force to Lift Objects

Object	Force Required to Lift on Earth (N)	Force Required to Lift on Planet X (N)	Force Required to Lift on Planet Y (N)	Mass (g)
1	20	8	4	2,000
2	7.5	3	1.5	750
3	12.5	5	2.5	1,250
4	5	2	1	500
5	25	10	5	2,500

Answer the questions.

1. Which of the three planets has the strongest gravitational pull? Explain.

_____

_____

2. Which of the three planets has the weakest gravitational pull? Explain.

_____

_____

GO ON TO THE NEXT PAGE

Unit 2: Keep on Moving!

How Much Force?, p. 2

3. Write a mathematical sentence that describes the relationship between the gravitational force on Earth and the gravitational force on planet Y.

_____

4. Write a mathematical sentence that describes the relationship between the gravitational force on Earth and the gravitational force on planet X.

_____

5. Write a mathematical sentence that describes the relationship between the gravitational force on planet X and on planet Y.

_____

6. Which object listed has the greatest mass on Earth? Explain.

_____

_____

7. List the objects in order, from the one having the greatest mass to the one having the least mass.

_____

8. Which object has four times the mass of which other object?

_____

Unit 2: Keep on Moving!

A Pendulum

"Tick, tock," sounds the grandfather clock. To and fro swings the weight far below. A grandfather clock has a heavy weight swinging at the end of a rod. The weight and rod together are an example of a pendulum. For centuries, pendulums have been used to run clocks. Do you know why?

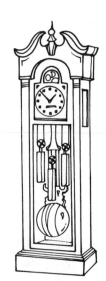

You can make a simple pendulum by tying a heavy object to one end of a piece of string. If you hold up the object by the opposite end of the string, you have made a pendulum. The heavy object is called the pendulum bob. When the pendulum bob is hanging straight, the pendulum is in its rest position.

What happens if you pull the pendulum from its rest position and then release it? The pendulum will swing back and forth. Each complete back-and-forth swing of the pendulum bob is called a cycle. The time it takes to complete one cycle is called the period of the pendulum. The motion of a pendulum is an example of simple harmonic motion—motion that repeats itself in a regular manner. You can also see simple harmonic motion for a short time in the bounces of a jack-in-the-box.

On each swing of a pendulum, the distance that the bob moves decreases. Finally, the bob will stop swinging. You will have to pull it from its rest position and then release it to start the pendulum moving again.

A pendulum stops swinging because air pushes against the bob as it moves and gravity pulls down on it. To keep a pendulum bob swinging, you have to push it a little on each swing. In a grandfather clock, the push is supplied by a wound-up spring. If you forget to wind the spring, the clock will eventually stop ticking.

In this activity, you and your partner will have a chance to investigate a pendulum. You will find out how you can change the motion of a pendulum.

 You will need:
   piece of string (70 cm long)
   heavy washer   meter stick
   pen or pencil   clock or watch that measures seconds

GO ON TO THE NEXT PAGE ▶

Unit 2: Keep on Moving!

A Pendulum, p. 2

1. Tightly tie the washer to one end of the string to make a pendulum.

2. Lay the meter stick along the pendulum. Measure a distance of 40 cm from the center of the washer. Mark this distance on the string with a pen or pencil. This distance is the length of the pendulum.

3. Hold the string at this mark above a tabletop so that the washer can swing freely. Have your partner pull the washer about 10 cm away from its rest position. Then have your partner release the washer.

4. Measure the time it takes in seconds for the washer to move through ten complete back-and-forth swings. Record in the table, under *Trial 1*, the time it took to complete the ten cycles. Repeat Steps 3 and 4 for two more trials.

5. Repeat Steps 2, 3, and 4 for pendulums with lengths of 20 cm and 10 cm.

Time For Ten Cycles (sec)

Length of Pendulum	Trial 1	Trial 2	Trial 3
40 cm			
20 cm			
10 cm			

Answer the questions.

1. Which object is the pendulum bob in this activity?

_____

2. How can you find the average period of each of these pendulums?

_____

_____

3. How does the length of a pendulum affect its period?

_____

_____

How Does Force Change Motion?

Forces can affect the motion of objects. Gravity is a force that acts on all objects in the universe. Gravity can affect the motion of a baseball that is thrown. Gravity causes an object to change direction as it falls.

Circular motion, such as a swinging ride at an amusement park, can be affected by the force of cables holding the cars. The collision of objects can affect motion, also. A collision can start motion, stop motion, change the speed of motion, or change the direction of motion.

Look at the diagrams below. Describe the force that is affecting the motion in each case.

1.

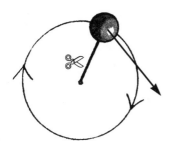

_____
_____
_____
_____

2.

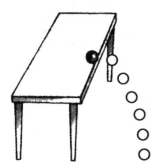

_____
_____
_____
_____

3.

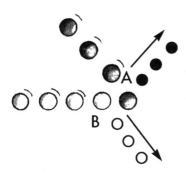

_____
_____
_____
_____

Unit 2: Keep on Moving!
Physical Science 5, SV 3764-X

Name _____ Date _____

Balanced and Unbalanced Forces

Some forces result in movement, and some do not. Two forces that are equal in size but opposite in direction are balanced forces. Balanced forces do not change the position of an object. To cause a change in motion, forces must be unbalanced. Unbalanced forces are opposite and unequal.

 You will need:

water	tissue paper
small paper cup	empty squeezable detergent bottle

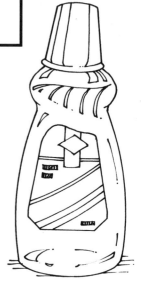

1. Moisten a small piece of tissue paper and shape it into a plug for the hole in the top of the bottle. Place it in the hole to plug the bottle.

2. Place the cup upside down over the bottle.

3. Squeeze the bottle as hard as you can. Observe what happens.

Answer the questions.

1. What two forces were acting to cause what you observed?

_____

_____

2. How did the two forces compare in their direction and size?

_____

_____

3. Could balanced forces have caused what you observed? Explain.

_____

_____

_____

Unit 2: Keep on Moving!
Physical Science 5, SV 3764-X

Name _____ Date _____

Friction

Friction is the force that resists motion between the surface of two objects that are touching. When objects slide over one another, the friction that results is called sliding friction. The friction produced by round objects such as wheels or balls is called rolling friction. Fluid friction is the force exerted by a fluid (a liquid or a gas) on an object moving through the fluid. The direction of the force is the opposite of the direction in which the object is moving.

Write *sliding*, *rolling*, or *fluid* to tell what kind of friction each picture shows.

1. _____   2. _____   3. _____

4. _____   5. _____   6. _____

Name _____ Date _____

How Do Lubricants Reduce Friction?

Lubricants are fluids, such as oil, that decrease friction between surfaces.

You will need:

large, smooth metal baking sheet
flat rubber eraser   stack of books
stopwatch   vegetable oil   paper towel

1. Stack the books. Use the baking sheet to make a ramp.

2. Place the eraser at the top of the ramp. Push it so it slides down the baking sheet. Time it with the stopwatch. You may have to push the eraser again if it stops. Record the time on the table below.

3. Pour a small amount of oil on the baking sheet. Use the paper towel to spread it evenly over the entire surface.

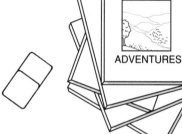

4. Repeat Step 2.

Answer the questions.

1. What effect did the oil have on the time for the eraser to slide down the ramp?

   _____

   _____

2. How did the fluid friction compare with the sliding friction?

   _____

   _____

3. Why do you think people use oil to lubricate the moving parts of machines?

   _____

   _____

Newton's Laws and Seatbelt Laws

No one goes to court to argue about Newton's first law of motion. It's not that kind of law. When you are riding in a car and someone brakes hard, your body continues to move forward. Young children can be thrown much farther than adults since they are so light. This is the reason that laws require children to ride buckled in car seats.

This activity demonstrates Newton's first law and the need for seatbelts.

 You will need:
a board at least 1 meter long
a toy car   books   ruler
1 small stone   1 heavy stone

1. Make a ramp by putting one end of the board on a pile of books. Put another book at the bottom of the ramp to act as a barrier.

2. Balance the small stone on top of the toy car. Let the car roll down the ramp.

3. Balance the large stone on top of the car and let the car roll down the ramp again.

Answer the questions.

1. How far was the small stone thrown when the car hit the barrier?

_____

2. How far was the large stone thrown?

_____

3. Do you better understand the need for safety seats for children? Do you think seatbelts are also important for adults? How would you explain this activity to someone else?

_____

_____

_____

Unit 2 Science Fair Ideas

A science fair project can help you to understand the world around you. Choose a topic that interests you. Then use the scientific method to develop your project. Here's an example:

1. **Problem:** What causes circular motion?

2. **Hypothesis:** Balanced forces create circular motion.

3. **Experimentation:** Materials: 12 cm-long plastic straw, 24 cm-long string, paper clip, pencil, ruler.

   - Tie one end of the string to the paper clip. Thread the loose end of the string through the straw. Tie the other end of the string to the pencil. Adjust the string so that the same lengths are on each end of the straw.

   - Hold the straw in one hand and the pencil still with the other hand. Swing the clip. As you swing it faster, let the pencil go.

4. **Observation:** The paper clip continues to swing in a circle after the hand releases the pencil.

5. **Conclusion:** When forces are balanced, an object in motion will move in a circle.

6. **Comparison:** The conclusion and the hypothesis agree.

7. **Presentation:** Prepare a presentation or a report to explain your results. Display your experiment so that other people can try it.

8. **Resources:** Tell the books you used to find background information. Tell who helped you to get the materials and set up the experiment.

Other Project Ideas

1. How do the brakes on a bike work? Do research on the forces that help brakes slow and stop a bike.

2. Many insects, such as ants, can carry more than their weight. Choose an insect and research to find how much force it can use to move objects.

Unit 2: Keep on Moving!

Unit 3 It Matters!

INTRODUCTION

By the fifth grade, students constantly question the whys and the hows of everything around them. Since they already understand the basic concepts of solids, gases, and liquids, they are now ready to explore the chemical compositions of compounds, including drawing models and formulas. Students also practice calculations to find the mass and volume of different objects. Finally, students determine acid, base, and neutral substances.

MATTER

Matter is all around. It is everything that we see and touch. Moreover, matter has mass, or weight, and takes up space. Matter is identified in three forms—solid, liquid, and gas. Though students can easily comprehend and recognize the properties of a solid and a liquid, it is generally difficult for them to understand that air is matter. Students begin to grasp this complex concept as they experiment with balloons and candles. (Energy is an example of something that is not matter and will be explored in Unit 3.)

Matter can be easily described by its properties, both physical and chemical. Physical properties describe how a substance looks, which includes color, shape, texture, melting point, and boiling point. By using their senses, students can describe what an item looks and feels like. Chemical properties tell how something reacts with another substance so that it changes in its appearance, taste, or smell. For example, iron reacts with oxygen and water to make a new substance—rust.

All matter is made up of tiny particles called *molecules.* Molecules are made up of even smaller particles called *atoms.* Molecules cannot be seen with a microscope, but students can understand a substance's properties by using their senses when performing simple experiments. If sugar is dissolved in water, the sugar cannot be seen; but it can be detected through taste because the water is sweet. By using the sense of smell, students can identify molecules of vinegar in air, a gas. To some degree, hearing can be used to sense molecules, because a smoke detector detects molecules of smoke in the air and buzzes to alert people to the potential danger.

 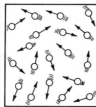 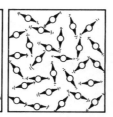

Solids

The state of matter is determined by the density of the molecules and how fast they move. In a solid, the molecules are attracted to each other and are tightly held together. The movement of the particles is limited—they vibrate only. Therefore, a solid has a definite shape and volume. For example, a rock has a certain shape. It can be broken into smaller pieces, but its molecules do not change. A solid's mass is measured in grams (g), a metric weight that is a scientific measurement standard.

Liquids

Liquids have a definite volume, but they take the shape of the container. The molecules in a liquid are not packed as tightly, so they can move about more freely and easily by sliding over each other. This movement is what makes a liquid take the shape of the container. When juice is in a carton, it takes the shape of the carton. Yet if poured into a glass, the juice takes the shape of the glass. The volume of a liquid is measured in milliliters (mL), the scientific standard measurement for liquid.

Gas

Gas is the third state of matter. It is harder for students to understand the properties of gas, because they cannot see it, nor have they had exposure to different kinds of gases. In a gas, the molecules are far apart and move very quickly and randomly in all directions. They bounce off each other when they collide. Gas has no definite shape or volume. Gas, therefore, expands to take the shape of a container. Gas is also measured in milliliters (mL).

MATTER CHANGES

All matter can change form, meaning it can change from one state to another. When matter changes, nothing is lost or gained—the molecules stay the same. The addition or the removal of heat causes the molecules to get closer or farther apart. Moreover, the greater the amount of heat, the faster the molecules move. These changes in the density and the speed of a substance's molecules cause the state of matter to change.

When a solid is heated, the molecules expand. The heat causes the speed and volume of molecules to change. They vibrate faster and slip out of position, resulting in the solid changing into a liquid. This process is called *melting,* and the point at which the solid changes to a liquid is called the *melting point*. All matter, including rocks, has a melting point. The most commonly recognized melting point (or freezing point) is that of water, which is 0° on the Celsius scale or 32° on the Fahrenheit scale. Even with this change, the structure of the molecules stays the same.

When a liquid is heated, the loose molecules continue to expand. The vibration increases, causing them to collide with each other and move in all directions. When the boiling point is reached, the liquid changes into a gas. The most commonly recognized boiling point is that of water. It boils at 100° Celsius or 212° Fahrenheit. This process is called *evaporation.* Again, the molecules stay the same; nothing is lost or gained when the matter changes states.

100

The removal of heat causes the reverse changes in matter. Through *condensation*, a gas is cooled, and the molecules contract. They stop colliding and return to their loosely packed state, thus becoming a liquid. If heat is removed to the point that a liquid reaches its freezing point, a liquid will become a solid. The molecules are densely packed and cannot slide around. In any of these changes, nothing is lost or gained; only the properties of matter change.

Students can easily experiment with changes in states by watching ice change to water and steam. Ice is a solid, but when heated to its freezing point, it turns to liquid water. No water is lost or gained in the process, and no molecules are changed. When more heat is added, the water changes to a gas called *water vapor* when it reaches its boiling point. The gas cannot be seen, because it has no color. Again, no water is lost or gained, and the molecules stay the same. If a spoon is held in the water vapor, the surface temperature of the spoon, which is room temperature, causes the water vapor to cool and condense back to liquid water. Likewise, by removing the heat and freezing the water, it changes states again to become ice.

Physical Changes

Matter can be changed in two ways, either in a physical change or in a chemical change. A physical change in matter is a change in which the molecules of a substance or substances do not change. There are three kinds of physical change. When matter changes states, as explained above, it is one kind of physical change.

A second kind of physical change takes place when a mixture is made. A mixture is a combination of substances in which the molecules of the substances diffuse evenly. Each substance retains its own properties and can be detected by the senses. None of the molecules is lost, gained, or changed. Moreover, a mixture can be separated by physical means, such as filtering, sorting, heating, or evaporating.

Each state of matter can make a kind of mixture. A fruit salad is an example of a solid mixture easily explained to students. Students can see and taste each piece of fruit. Sorting the fruit chunks is possible. Gas can also be mixed with another substance to form a mixture. The scent of a flower mixes with air so that you can smell the flower several feet away. You use your sense of smell to become aware of the scent. A liquid can also be a made into a mixture. Often a solid is dissolved into a liquid. This kind of mixture is called a *solution*. It is hard to separate the parts, but it can be done. Lemonade is a good example to explain a solution. Water, lemon, and sugar are mixed together. Even though lemonade does not look like a mixture, the ingredients can be separated. The lemon can be filtered out. The water can evaporate, leaving crystals of sugar.

A third kind of physical change takes place when the shape of a substance is changed through cutting, ripping, or grinding. A log can be cut into many pieces. What remains are sawdust and cut logs. The molecules of the log itself have not changed.

Chemical Changes

When the molecules of a substance change and it exhibits new properties, a chemical change has taken place. A new substance is always made in a chemical change, but molecules are never lost. Even though new molecules are made, the same number of atoms exists. Energy, generally in the form of heat, causes the atoms in molecules to break down to form different molecules. Baking is a common example of a chemical change. Sugar, milk, eggs, and flour are combined to make a cake batter mixture. When heat is added, a chemical change takes place to turn the ingredients into a cake. Chemical changes also occur in the human body. Through chemical changes, food and oxygen react in the body's cells to create energy to make the body work.

When two or more elements combine in a chemical change, a compound forms. For example, two hydrogen atoms and one oxygen atom make water. A model can be drawn to show the makeup. Chemistry uses letter symbols for elements. The formula for water is H_2O. It shows the number of atoms and the elements in it.

hydrogen + oxygen → water

Acids and Bases

Compounds can be divided into categories of acids, bases, and neutrals. Acids have a bitter or sour taste, whereas bases have a soapy feel. Lemon juice, carbonated drinks, and vinegar are examples of acids. Soap and ammonia are bases.

Litmus paper or pH paper is used to determine the classification of a substance. With blue litmus paper, an acid will change the paper to pink. With pink litmus, however, an acid will not change its color. The reverse is true for a base. A base will turn pink litmus to blue, while not affecting the color of blue paper. A neutral substance will not change the color of either paper.

Crystals

A crystal is a solid whose particles are arranged in a pattern. They are often formed when a solution is saturated, meaning a liquid is full of a solute so that no more can be dissolved. Crystals can form when a melted substance full of solute cools, when a saturated substance evaporates, or when a hot, saturated substance cools. Salt is a basic kind of crystal most students will recognize.

Properties of Matter

Everything we see, touch, taste, and smell is matter. Matter is anything that has mass and takes up space. We can tell different substances, or objects of matter, apart by their characteristics, or properties. Some of these properties are color, taste, and odor. Some properties of a substance always stay the same. For example, the color, taste, and smell of an orange are the same whether the orange is small or large, whole or sliced.

Other properties that identify matter include its melting temperature, freezing temperature, and its ability to conduct electricity. These properties change. Water changes because its properties can change.

1. Describe what matter is.

_____

_____

2. What are some properties of matter?

_____

_____

3. Describe an orange according to its properties.

_____

_____

_____

Measuring Units

Another way that matter can be described is by measurement. You use measurements in almost everything you do. When everyone agrees to use the same units of measurement, they are using standard units. Scientists from around the world have adopted the International System of Units, or SI, for a standard of measurement. People use these standard units to make all kinds of measurements every day. For example, cooking requires measuring volume, or the amount of space something takes up. When you measure the amount of matter in an object, you are measuring mass. People often confuse mass with weight, which is a measure of the force of gravity pulling on an object. Weight varies with the gravitational force on an object, but mass remains the same.

1. Why do we measure using standard units instead of measuring with any kind of units?

   _____

   _____

   _____

   _____

2. Complete the chart by filling in the symbol for the appropriate SI unit. Use additional resources if you need to.

Unit Measurement

	SI Unit	SI Symbol
Length		
Mass		
Volume of solids		
Temperature		

A Matter of Units

Kuang plans to visit his friend Joan at her new school. He has his bicycle all packed up and ready to go. But when he looks at the directions Joan has written, Kuang realizes he has a major problem! Joan expressed each unit of measurement in metric units. Kuang's odometer uses English Standard units. In order for Kuang to reach his destination, he needs to convert the metric units to English Standard units.

Use this conversion chart to help Kuang find his way, based on Joan's directions, given below the chart.

Conversion Chart

When You Know	Multiply By	To Find
millimeters	0.04	inches
centimeters	0.4	inches
meters	1.1	yards
kilometers	0.6	miles

Directions to Joan's School

Distance in Metric Units

Distance in English Standard Units

1. Ride to the end of your block. Turn right on Main Street. Continue on Main Street for 84 meters.

    84 meters = _____ yards

2. Turn left onto Poplar Ave. Ride straight on Poplar Ave. for 3 kilometers.

    3 kilometers = _____ miles

3. At the fork in the road, bear right onto Elm St. Ride straight on Elm St. for 122 meters.

    122 meters = _____ yards

4. Turn left onto School Lane. The school is located 58 meters from the corner.

    58 meters = _____ yards

GO ON TO THE NEXT PAGE ➤

Unit 3: It Matters!

Name _____   Date _____

A Matter of Units, p. 2

Conversion Chart

When You Know	Multiply By	To Find
Units of Length		
inches	25	millimeters
feet	30	centimeters
yards	0.9	meters
miles	1.6	kilometers
Units of Mass		
ounces	28	grams
pounds	0.45	kilograms
Units of Volume		
pints	0.47	liters
quarts	0.95	liters
gallons	3.8	liters

Use the conversion chart above to answer the questions.

1. Judd is 4 feet tall. How many centimeters tall is he?

_____

2. A can of soup holds 28 ounces. How many grams does the can hold?

_____

3. Mrs. Wilson purchased 6 yards of fabric. How many meters of the fabric did she buy?

_____

4. The distance between two cities is 42 miles. What is this distance in kilometers?

_____

5. Rita bought three containers of soda. If each container holds 2 quarts, how many liters of soda did Rita buy?

_____

Name _____   Date _____

States of Matter

Matter can also be found in solid, liquid, and gas states, or phases. Some matter can go through all three phase changes as a result of heating or cooling. Water, for example, forms a solid at freezing temperatures, and when heated, melts into a liquid. As a liquid, water can change into a gas through evaporation and can once again, through cooling, become a liquid by condensation.

Answer the questions.

1. In the boxes below, show which is the solid, liquid, or gas by labeling each.

a. _____   **b.** _____   **c.** _____

2. Explain why condensation forms on a glass containing a cold drink.

_____

_____

_____

3. Explain how evaporation occurs.

_____

_____

_____

Molecules in Matter

The three states of matter are solids, liquids, and gases. Molecules are the smallest parts of a substance. In solids, molecules are packed tightly together, vibrating slightly. For this reason, solids retain their shape. In liquids, molecules are packed less tightly; they slide over each other. Therefore, water has the characteristics of size and movement. In gases, molecules bump against each other, moving wildly and quickly in all directions. Gas does not have its own shape and must take the shape of its container.

Look at the pictures. Tell which is a picture of the molecules in a *solid*, *liquid*, or *gas*.

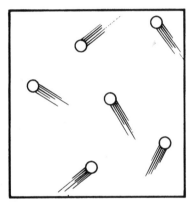 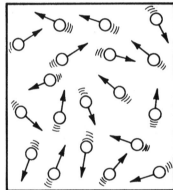 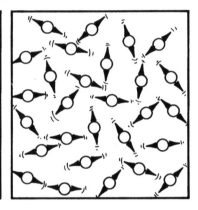

1. _____   **2.** _____   **3.** _____

Answer the questions.

4. In which kind of matter do the molecules move the fastest?

_____

5. In which kind of matter do the molecules vibrate?

_____

6. Compare the movement of molecules in a solid with the movement of molecules in a liquid.

_____

_____

Unit 3: It Matters!

Name _____   Date _____

Ice Cube Meltdown

Do you prefer to drink fruit juice with or without ice? Does adding ice cubes affect the taste of fruit juice? In this activity you will learn something that will help you answer these questions.

 You will need:

3-4 ice cubes	beaker or clear plastic cup
clock	grease pencil or marker

1. This activity will take two days to complete. Record all your observations on the table on page 110.

Day 1

2. Place the ice cubes in the beaker. Record the date and time on the table on page 110.

3. Observe the size and shape of the ice cubes. Record your observations on the table.

4. After 30 minutes, observe the ice cubes again. Write the date, the time, and your observations on the table.

5. Record the time at which the ice cubes have melted completely. Use the grease pencil to mark the water level on the container. Log the time and your observations on the table.

Day 2

6. Observe the container. Mark the water level on the container. Log the date, the time, and your observations on the table.

GO ON TO THE NEXT PAGE ➡

Ice Cube Meltdown, p. 2

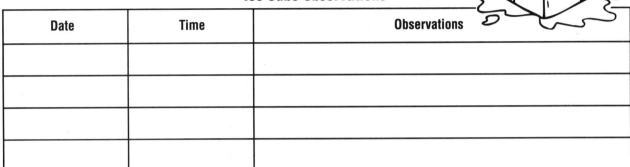

Ice Cube Observations

Date	Time	Observations

Answer the questions.

1. In what state of matter was the water when you put the ice cubes into the container? How do you know this?

   _____

2. What state of matter did the water then change into? How do you know this?

   _____

3. What caused this change of state?

   _____

4. How did the water level of the container change between day 1 and day 2?

   _____

5. What caused this change in water level?

   _____

6. What do you infer would happen to the taste of fruit juice if ice were added?

   _____

   _____

   _____

Unit 3: It Matters!

Name _____   Date _____

Measuring Mass

A balance is used to measure a solid object's mass, or weight. Balances have two pans. In one pan you place the object you want to measure. In the other you place the gram (g) weights, the metric units used by scientists to measure mass.

Measuring Mass

Object	Mass (g)

 You will need:

balance   gram weights   4 or 5 objects

1. Make sure the empty pans are balanced. They are in balance if the pointer is at the middle mark on the base. If the pointer is not at this mark, move the slider to the right or left.

2. Place one object in a pan. The pointer will move toward the pan that is empty.

3. Choose weights to place carefully in the other pan. The pointer will move back toward the middle. When the pointer is in the middle, the pans are balanced. Add the numbers on the gram weights. The total is the mass of the object.

4. Fill in the chart as you go.

5. Repeat with the other objects.

Answer the questions.

1. Why must the pointer be in the middle before you begin?

_____

2. How do you find the mass of an object once the balance is equal?

_____

3. List your items in order from the least mass to the most mass.

_____

Measuring Volume

Volume is how much space an object takes up. For objects that have a regular shape with straight sides, like a box, you use a ruler and this formula: *length x width x height = volume*. The scientific unit to measure volume is cubic centimeters (cm^3). For objects that have an irregular shape, like a rock, you will need to use a measuring cup of water and the scientific unit of milliliters (mL). One cubic centimeter equals one milliliter.

Measuring Volume

Object	Volume (cm^3 or mL)

✔ **You will need:**

metric ruler   measuring cup
water   string
4 or 5 objects

1. For the objects with straight sides, use the ruler to measure their length, width, and height. Find their volume by multiplying these numbers together. Record the volume in the table. (Remember to use the correct scientific unit.)

2. For objects with irregular sides, fill a measuring cup half full with water. Note the water level. Tie a string around the object and lower it into the cup. Be sure the object is totally under water. Subtract the first water level from the second. The difference is the object's volume. Record the volume in the table.

Answer the questions.

1. Which method would you use to find the volume of a fish tank? Explain.

_____

_____

2. Which method would you use to find the volume of a set of keys? Explain.

_____

_____

3. List your items in order from the least volume to the most volume.

_____

Unit 3: It Matters!

Measuring Density

The density of an object tells you how much mass is in a certain volume. To find the density, you need to know the mass and volume of the object. You then divide the mass of the object by its volume.

$$\text{Density} = \frac{\text{Mass}}{\text{Volume}}$$

The units of density are grams per milliliter or grams per cubic centimeter. These units are written as g/mL and g/cc. You can compare densities of different materials.

 You will need:
balance with gram masses   water
metric measuring cup
materials to measure, such as milk, corn oil, and syrup

1. Using the balance, find the mass of the measuring cup. What is its mass? _____

2. Using the measuring cup, measure exactly 100 mL of water. Find the mass of the water and the cup together. What is it? _____

3. To find the mass of the water, subtract the mass of the measuring cup from the total mass of the cup and the water. What is the mass of the water? _____

4. Now you can find the density of water. Divide the mass of the water by the volume of water. What is the density?

_____

5. Find the density of other liquids, such as milk and corn oil. Fill in the chart below.

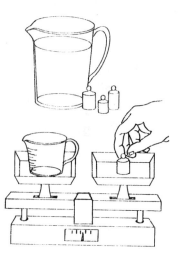

Measurement

Name of Liquid	Mass of Measuring Cup	Mass of Liquid and Measuring Cup	Mass of Liquid	Volume	Density
water					

Unit 3: It Matters!
Physical Science 5, SV 3764-X

Finding Density

The density of an object tells us how much mass is in a particular volume. Here is how to find the density of an object: Divide the mass of the object by its volume. For example, 50 grams of water has a volume of 50 milliliters. To find the density, divide 50 g by 50 mL.

$$50 \text{ g} \div 50 \text{ mL} = 1 \text{ g/mL}$$

Therefore, water has a density of 1 g/mL.

A. Find the density of the following objects. Do your calculations on a separate sheet of paper. Your answer will be in grams per milliliter (g/mL) or grams per cubic centimeter (g/cc). These are written g/mL or g/cc. Write the answers on the lines below.

1. A coil of copper wire has a mass of 900 grams and a volume of 100 cubic centimeters. _____

2. A bar of gold has a mass of 1,900 grams and a volume of 100 cubic centimeters. _____

3. A sample of mercury has a mass of 260 grams and a volume of 20 milliliters. _____

4. A pile of coins has a mass of 540 g and a volume of 60 cubic centimeters. _____

B. Rebecca bought 1,000 g of aluminum nails. She decided to find their density. She put the nails in a container of water. The water level rose 370 mL. What is the volume of the nails? _____

What is the density of the aluminum nails? _____

Name _____ Date _____

Liquid Matter

All matter has properties, or characteristics. For example, all matter has mass, volume, and density. Liquid matter has another interesting property. The small particles of a liquid attract each other. The strength of the attraction varies from liquid to liquid. Those that have particles that attract each other strongly, spread out less. Measuring this property, in fact, can help you identify liquids.

✔ **You will need:**
plastic wrap   paper towels   eyedropper
liquids to test (water, vegetable oil, honey, alcohol, lemon juice, liquid soap, syrup, milk)

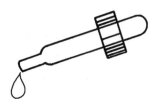

1. Use the eyedropper to put one drop of water on the plastic wrap. Look at the drop from the side. Draw its shape in the chart. Add three more drops to the first. Draw the new shape.

2. Rinse out the dropper and dry it well. Test other liquids in the same way. Be sure you rinse and dry the dropper after each trial. Record your results. Do all the drops look the same? _____

Explain. _____

_____

Liquid	Shape of One Drop	Shape of Four Drops	Number of Squares Covered
Water			

GO ON TO THE NEXT PAGE ➡

Unit 3: It Matters!

Liquid Matter, p. 2

3. Will 20 drops of oil spread over the same area as 20 drops of water? To find out, place plastic wrap over the grid shown below. Place 20 drops of water on the dot in the center of the grid. Count how many squares the water covers either totally or partially. Record this number in the chart.

4. With a paper towel, wipe the plastic. Now place 20 drops of oil on the center of the grid. Count how many squares the oil covers. Record the number in the chart. Which covered more squares—oil or water?

_____

5. Test the rest of the liquids in the same way. Which liquid spreads out the most? Which liquids spread the least?

_____

6. Compare the shape of one drop of the liquid that spread the most with one that spread the least.

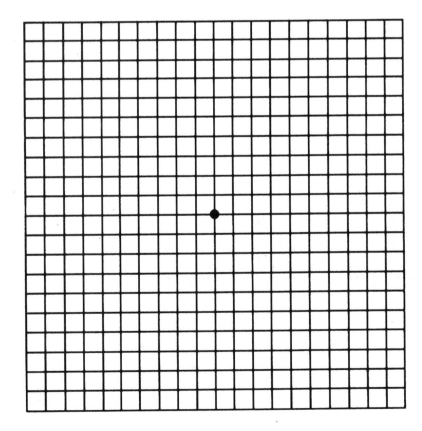

Changes in Matter

Matter is made up of basic units. Matter can be combined, separated, mixed, and altered. The smallest building block of matter that retains the properties of matter is the atom. A single crystal of salt or grain of rice is made up of millions of atoms. Atoms are too small to be seen, except with very powerful microscopes.

An element is made up of only one kind of atom. Few of the things you see around you are pure elements. Wood, plastic, and steel are made of molecules that consist of many kinds of atoms.

A substance made of two or more elements chemically combined is called a compound. When two or more atoms combine, they form a molecule. A molecule is the smallest particle of matter that consists of more than one atom.

Underline the best answer.

1. The smallest building block of matter is . . .
   a. a molecule.   **b.** an element.   **c.** an atom.   **d.** a compound.

2. . . . is made up of only one kind of atom.
   a. A molecule   **b.** An element   **c.** An atom   **d.** A compound

3. . . . is a substance made of two or more elements chemically combined.
   a. A molecule   **b.** An element   **c.** An atom   **d.** A compound

4. When two or more atoms combine, they form . . .
   a. a molecule.   **b.** an element.   **c.** an atom.   **d.** a compound.

Kinds of Matter

Your teacher will divide the class into teams of three for a kind of scavenger hunt. Your team will search the classroom and list all the substances in it. But there is a catch. You have to classify each substance under one of the headings shown below. Your teacher will help you get started by asking the class for an example of one item for each heading. The team with the most accurate list wins!

Elements	Compounds	Mixtures

Unit 3: It Matters!

Molecule Detectors

Your senses can often tell you when molecules travel in the air or through a liquid. For example, you can smell hot soup when molecules of the soup reach your nose. When you add food coloring to water, you see the color as it moves through the water.

Look at the pictures below. In each one something is happening that causes molecules to travel through air or a liquid. On the first line under each picture, write which sense would tell you that molecules moved from one place to another. On the second line write *air* or *liquid* to tell where molecules have moved.

1.

_____

_____

2.

_____

_____

3.

_____

_____

4.

_____

_____

5.

_____

_____

6.

_____

_____

Name _____   Date _____

Moving Molecules

A. Molecules are so tiny that they can pass through the tiny holes in the fabric of a balloon. To show this, you will need a balloon.

1. Blow up the balloon and tie the neck tightly. Set it aside for a week.

2. Look at the balloon again. How has it changed? Explain.

_____

_____

_____

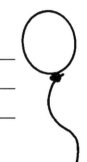

B. Molecules in liquids move from place to place. Find out whether molecules move faster in warm water or cold water.

 You will need:

| 2 clear plastic cups | food coloring |
| watch with a second hand | water |

1. Fill one cup with very warm water. Fill the other with cold water.

2. Work with a partner. Put two drops of food coloring in each cup at the same time. Write your starting time in the table. Then time how long it takes for the food coloring to spread in the cups. Record your ending time, too.

Molecule Movement

Time	Warm Water	Cold Water
Starting Time		
Finishing Time		

Answer the questions.

1. How long did it take for the color to spread in the warm water? _____

2. How long did it take for the color to spread in the cold water? _____

3. Which took longer? Explain. _____

_____

Unit 3: It Matters!

Physical Science 5, SV 3764-X

Name _____ Date _____

Heat and Molecules

We know that all matter is made of tiny particles called
molecules. These particles are in constant motion. Scientists
know that heat is a form of energy. As an object becomes hotter,
its atoms and molecules move faster. You can determine how
hot something is by taking its temperature. Temperature is the
measure of the average kinetic energy, or energy of movement,
of the atoms and molecules in a substance or an object.

1. How is heat related to temperature?

_____

_____

_____

2. What happens to solids, liquids, and gases when they are heated?

_____

_____

_____

3. How does a solid change when heat is added?

_____

_____

4. How does a gas change when heat is reduced?

_____

_____

Name _____ Date _____

Mixtures

In a mixture, the parts keep their properties, even though the parts are mixed together. A solution is a mixture in which the composition is the same throughout. A suspension is a solution in which one of the parts is a liquid. Suspensions are very common in everyday life.

When you are making a gelatin dessert mold, you are making another type of mixture. The gelatin in the dessert is a mixture called a colloid. In a colloid, the particles do not dissolve, but they are so small that they do not settle out. They remain suspended because they are constantly moving.

 Underline the best answer.

1. In . . . the parts keep their own properties.

   a. a suspension   **b.** a solution   **c.** a mixture   **d.** a colloid

2. . . . are mixtures in which the composition is the same throughout.

   a. Suspensions   **b.** Solutions   **c.** Mixtures   **d.** Colloids

3. . . . is a mixture in which one of the parts is a liquid.

   a. A suspension   **b.** A solution   **c.** A mixture   **d.** A colloid

4. . . . is a mixture in which the particles do not settle out.

   a. A suspension   **b.** A solution   **c.** A mixture   **d.** A colloid

5. Describe what the solvent and solute of a solution are.

_____

_____

_____

_____

Changes in Matter

There are two ways matter can change—chemically and physically. When elements combine to form a compound, a chemical change occurs. In a chemical change, a new chemical is formed from another type of matter. Burning charcoal is an example of a chemical change.

A physical change in matter is a change in matter that does not form a new chemical. Examples of physical changes are boiling, dissolving, evaporating, and freezing.

1. Explain the difference between a chemical change and a physical change.

_____

_____

_____

_____

2. List some clues that a chemical change has occurred.

_____

_____

_____

_____

3. Identify each example as a chemical change or a physical change.

Example	Type of Change
a. Cutting strawberries	
b. Cooking a hot dog	

Physical or Chemical Change?

Look at each picture. Decide what kind of change it shows.
Write _physical_ under each picture that shows a physical change.
Write _chemical_ under each picture that shows a chemical change.

1. _____

2. _____

3. _____

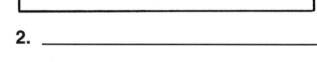

4. _____

5. _____

6. _____

Compounds

A compound results when two or more elements combine chemically. As a result, you end up with something you didn't have before. Rust is a compound. Rust results from the combining of atoms of the element oxygen in air with atoms of the element iron.

Water is also a compound. Each molecule of the compound water is made up of two atoms of hydrogen and one atom of oxygen. Hydrogen and oxygen are gases, but when they combine as H_2O, they form the clear liquid water.

Another example of a compound is salt. Salt is made up of the elements sodium and chlorine. As an element, sodium is a solid that is dangerous to handle because it can burst into flames. Chlorine is a poisonous gas. But when sodium and chlorine are combined chemically in the ratio of one to one, they form salt (NaCl), a white crystal that is safe to handle and eat.

1. Explain the difference between a mixture and a compound.

_____

_____

_____

_____

2. Explain how the compound water is formed.

_____

_____

_____

_____

Name _____ Date _____

How Can You Make a Model of a Compound?

A compound is a substance formed when two or more elements, or atoms, are chemically combined. A scientific model or drawing shows the way atoms are joined to make different compounds. A compound can also be written as a formula, a number that shows how many of each atom are present. The table below identifies some compounds, showing both a drawing and the formula for each.

Compound	Formula	Model
Hydrogen peroxide	H_2O_2	(H)(O)(O)(H)
Carbon dioxide	CO_2	(O)(C)(O)
Ammonia	NH_3	(H)(N)(H)(H)
Hydrogen chloride	HCl	(H)(Cl)

✔ You will need:

5 colors of modeling clay
toothpicks   paper   pencil

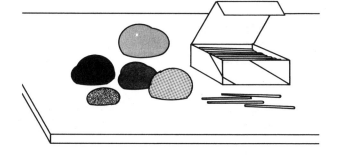

1. Choose one of the compounds from the table. Look at the elements in each. Compare the size of the atoms.

2. Choose a color of clay for each element. Make balls in comparable sizes to the drawing on the table.

3. Join the clay balls with toothpicks, making sure they are placed in the same spot as the drawing on the table shows.

4. Make a label for your model. Include the name of the compound and the formula. Make a table to show which colors stand for each element.

       Unit 3: It Matters!

Physical Science 5, SV 3764-X

Models and Symbols

To help them understand how molecules are built, chemists make models. Look at the model of the water molecule.

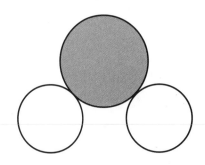

How many atoms of hydrogen are in it?

_____

How many atoms of oxygen are in it?

_____

Chemists also use letter symbols to stand for molecules. Water is written as H_2O. The H stands for hydrogen. The 2 after the H means there are 2 atoms of hydrogen. The O stands for oxygen. The number *1* is never written after a chemical symbol. If no number is written, you know there is only 1 atom of that kind in the molecule. There is only 1 atom of oxygen in a molecule of water.

Below are the letter symbols and models of several elements. Study the symbol and model for each element. Then look at the pictures of the molecules. Use these symbols to write the names of the molecules shown.

  H — hydrogen   O — oxygen   C — carbon   N — nitrogen

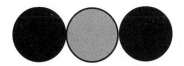
carbon dioxide

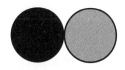
carbon monoxide

oxygen

1. _____   2. _____   3. _____

GO ON TO THE NEXT PAGE ➤

Unit 3: It Matters!

     Physical Science 5, SV 3764-X

Models and Symbols, p. 2

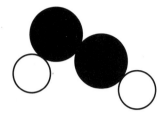

hydrogen peroxide

4. _____

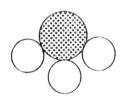

ammonia

5. _____

hydrogen

6. _____

nitrogen dioxide

7. _____

8. Which of the molecules shown above are elements? Explain.

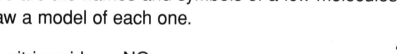

_____

_____

Here are the names and symbols of a few molecules.
Draw a model of each one.

9. nitric oxide — NO

10. nitrous oxide — N_2O

11. methane gas — CH_4

Word Equations

Chemists have a special way of writing about chemical changes. They write word equations instead of complete sentences. In a word equation, a few words and math symbols tell what happens. For example, here is a word equation that tells what happens when an iron nail rusts.

iron + oxygen → iron oxide

It is read this way: "Iron and oxygen become iron oxide." The name *iron oxide* tells you two things. It tells you that iron is part of the compound. The word *oxide* tells you that oxygen also is part of the compound. The arrow means "becomes."

What do these word equations say?

1. mercury + oxygen → mercuric oxide

_____

2. carbon + oxygen → carbon dioxide

_____

3. hydrogen + oxygen → water

_____

4. Do the word equations above tell about building up compounds or breaking down compounds?

_____

GO ON TO THE NEXT PAGE

Unit 3: It Matters!

Word Equations, p. 2

Word equations can be used to show that a compound may be broken down into its elements. For example, here is a word equation that tells about salt. Another name for salt is sodium chloride.

sodium chloride → sodium + chlorine

It is read this way:
"Sodium chloride becomes sodium and chlorine."

What do these word equations say?

1. water → hydrogen + oxygen

_____

2. mercuric oxide → mercury + oxygen

_____

3. iron sulfide → iron + sulfur

_____

Complete these word equations:

4. calcium chloride → _____ + chlorine

5. _____ + oxygen → zinc oxide

6. _____ + chlorine → hydrogen chloride

7. hydrogen iodide → _____ + iodine

Secret Writing

Iodine will combine with starch to form a new compound. Iodine is reddish-orange. Starch is white. The new compound is dark blue. You can use this information about iodine and starch to send a secret message.

You will need:

cornstarch	spoon	water	shallow pan
waxed paper	iodine	measuring spoons	
measuring cup	white paper	bowl	toothpick

NOTE: THIS EXPERIMENT MUST BE DONE WITH AN ADULT. IODINE IS POISONOUS.

1. In the bowl, mix together a tablespoon of cornstarch and a tablespoon of water. Stir until the mixture is smooth.

2. Use the toothpick as a pen. Use the cornstarch mixture as ink. Write a secret message to a classmate on a piece of paper. Have your classmate write a secret message to you. Let the messages dry.

3. While your messages are drying, mix a tablespoon of iodine with one cup of water in the pan.

4. When the "ink" is dry, look at your message. Is it easy to read? _____ Trade messages with your classmate.

5. Dip the paper into the iodine mixture. Make sure the writing is completely covered. Wait a few minutes. What do you see?

_____

6. Remove the paper. Place it on a piece of waxed paper to dry. Does the message disappear when the paper dries? Explain. _____

_____

_____

The iodine combined with starches in both the paper and the cornstarch mixture. There are different kinds and amounts of starches in the paper and the cornstarch. Therefore, they did not turn the same shade of blue when they reacted with the iodine.

Making Carbon Dioxide

Carbon dioxide is a compound made from carbon and oxygen. When carbon and oxygen are combined, a chemical change occurs. The compound carbon dioxide is formed. You can make carbon dioxide by combining baking soda and vinegar. These two substances contain the elements carbon and oxygen. When baking soda and vinegar are mixed, the carbon and oxygen join to form carbon dioxide.

Make carbon dioxide and learn about its density.

 You will need:

large jar	spoon	unpopped popcorn kernels
water	baking soda	measuring spoons
vinegar	measuring cup	

1. Pour 350 mL of water into the jar. Add 2 teaspoons of baking soda. Stir until the baking soda dissolves.

2. Add about 30 kernels of popcorn.
What happens? _____
What does this tell you about the density of popcorn?

_____

3. Pour 45 mL of vinegar into the water. Stir gently. What happens?

_____

These bubbles are carbon dioxide gas. What do the bubbles do?

_____

What does this tell you about the density of carbon dioxide?

_____

4. Watch the popcorn for a few minutes.

What happens? _____

_____

What does this tell you about the density of the popcorn-bubble combination? _____

Name _____ Date _____

How Can You Separate Compounds?

To separate the color dye compound in felt-tip markers, you will need various colored felt-tip markers, a paper towel, a baby food jar, a pair of scissors, and water.

1. Cut out circles from white paper towels. The circles should be 10 cm in diameter. Cut a narrow tail into the center of each circle as shown in Figure 1. Put a spot of color from a marker at the top of the tail. Use a different color on each circle.

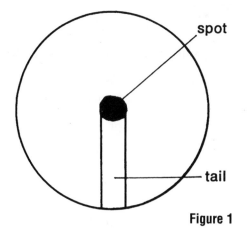

Figure 1

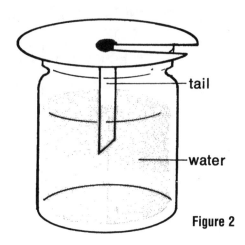

Figure 2

2. Bend the tail of one circle downward. Set it in a baby food jar full of water as shown in Figure 2. Watch the dye spread.

3. Write the color of the marker and the color or colors of the dye compounds in the table below.

Dye Compounds

Color of Marker	Dye Compounds in Marker

Unit 3: It Matters!

Physical Science 5, SV 3764-X

Name _____   Date _____

Crystals

Crystals are particles that are arranged in an orderly pattern. Crystals come in all sizes. When liquid substances freeze, the temperature around them affects the size of their crystals.

 You will need:

3 small glass bottles or jars   moth flakes (paradichlorobenzene)
ice cubes   small pan   water   hotplate

NOTE: THIS EXPERIMENT MUST BE DONE WITH AN ADULT.

1. Fill each jar with moth flakes. Pour water into the pan until it is 3 cm deep. Set the jars in the water.

2. Heat the water on the hotplate until you see the moth flakes begin to melt.

3. After the moth flakes are all melted, take two jars out of the hot water. Put one in a bowl with cold water. Then add ice cubes to the cold water. Leave the other jar on the table. Leave the third jar in the hot water, but not on the hotplate.

4. When all the liquid moth flakes have crystallized, compare the size of the crystals in the three jars from largest to smallest crystals.

 Answer the questions.

1. In which jar did crystals form first? _____

2. In which jar did the crystals form last? _____

3. In which jars did the largest crystals form? the smallest? _____

_____

4. In which jar did the liquid cool the fastest? slowest? _____

_____

5. How does the rate of cooling affect the size of the crystals? _____

_____

_____

Unit 3: It Matters!

Common Crystal Shapes

This activity will familiarize you with two common crystal shapes. Cut out the diagrams. Fold along all the lines. Glue each lettered tab under its matching edge.

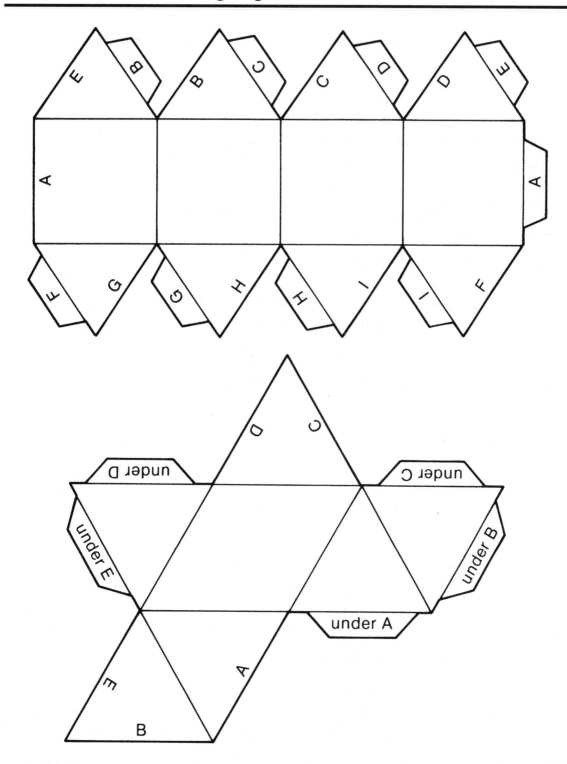

Unit 3: It Matters!

Physical Science 5, SV 3764-X

Name _____   Date _____

Acids and Bases

Compounds can be divided into two groups—acids and bases. There are many kinds of acids and bases in your home and school. Litmus paper is a way to test a substance chemically to discover which compound it is. Litmus paper comes in colors of blue and pink. A substance that is a base will change pink litmus to blue. A substance that is an acid will change blue litmus to pink. If both strips stay the same color, then the substance is neutral. It is neither a base nor an acid.

✔ **You will need:**

pink and blue litmus paper	lemon juice	milk
carbonated drink	dish soap	marker
small paper cups	sugar water	

1. Label each cup with the name of the substance. Pour a small amount of each into the cup.

2. Dip a strip of blue litmus into the first substance. Did it change color? Record your findings on the table.

3. Dip a strip of pink litmus into the same cup. Did it change color? Record your findings on the table.

4. Record whether each substance is a base, an acid, or a neutral in the last column of the table.

Testing Household Substances

Material	Reaction to blue litmus paper	Reaction to pink litmus paper	What substance is
Lemon juice			
Milk			
Dish soap			
Sugar water			
Carbonated drink			

Red Cabbage Indicator

Litmus paper is used to tell whether a substance is an acid or a base. Because it can indicate properties, litmus paper is called an indicator. Other chemicals can be used as indicators, too. For example, methyl orange turns red in the presence of an acid. It turns yellow in the presence of a strong base.

You don't need special chemicals, however, to make an indicator for acids and bases. You can use the juice from red cabbage. To get red cabbage juice, buy cooked red cabbage in a can or jar, and drain off the juice. Use red cabbage juice as an indicator.

✔ You will need:

measuring cup	measuring spoon	baking soda
clean plastic cup	vinegar	red cabbage juice

Optional: other natural juices, such as carrot, beet, grape, and cherry

1. Pour some red cabbage juice into the plastic cup. Add a pinch of baking soda. What happens? _____

_____

This color appears when cabbage juice mixes with a base.

2. Add vinegar. What happens? _____

_____

This color appears when cabbage juice mixes with an acid.

3. Find out whether other natural juices can be used as indicators for acids and bases. Test other juices. Add your results to the table.

Acids and Bases in Fruit and Vegetable Juices

Indicator	Color It Turns in an Acid	Color It Turns in a Base
red cabbage juice		

Unit 3: It Matters!

Physical Science 5, SV 3764-X

Name _____   Date _____

Acids and Bases Around the House

Now that you know about acids and bases, can you solve these mysteries?

A. The Refrigerator Robber silently opened the refrigerator door. As the light came on, he glimpsed a pitcher of fruit juice. He grabbed it and eased the door shut. The sour taste told him he had grabbed grapefruit juice.
1. Is grapefruit juice an acid or a base? _____

B. Cathy Chemist washed her hands with soap and water. Then she picked up a piece of litmus paper. It turned blue!
2. Why? _____

_____

_____

C. Helpful Harry was helping his mother clean out the kitchen cabinets. He knocked a bottle off the shelf! Horrors! It hit the counter and broke! Oh, woe! The baking soda is getting soaked! It's bubbling all over the place!
3. The liquid in the broken bottle must be: _____

_____

_____

Does the Amount of Matter Change After a Chemical Reaction?

When matter changes form in a chemical reaction, it will look, smell, and feel different. However, nothing is lost or gained. It should have the same mass.

You will need:

| baking soda | small funnel | teaspoon | balloon |
| empty pill bottle | vinegar | balance scale | gram weights |

1. Pour one teaspoon of baking soda through the funnel into the balloon.

2. Fill the bottle half full with vinegar.

3. Pull the opening of the balloon over the mouth of the bottle.

4. Put the balloon and bottle on one side of the balance scale. Add weights to the other side until the balance is level.

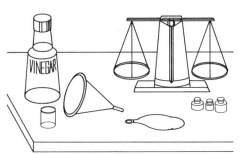

5. Remove the balloon and bottle from the scale. Pour the baking soda from the balloon into the bottle of vinegar. Observe what happens.

6. Repeat Step 4.

Answer the questions.

1. What happened when you mixed the baking soda and the vinegar in Step 5? _____

2. Did the balance remain level after replacing the balloon and bottle on the balance in Step 6? _____

3. Was the amount of matter the same both before and after the chemical reaction? Explain. _____

_____

Name _____   Date _____

Matter Word Scramble

Unscramble the words in the box. Then use the
words to complete the sentences below. To help you,
the first letter in each word has been underlined.

Word List

cluelo<u>me</u>	ss<u>b</u>ea	emulo<u>v</u>	mo<u>at</u>	s<u>ai</u>dc
tiesper<u>p</u>ro	<u>d</u>yetins	la<u>c</u>ihemc	dupmno<u>c</u>o	hm<u>c</u>tssei

1. Common compounds that turn blue litmus paper to pink are

   _____.

2. A water molecule contains one _____ of
   oxygen and two of hydrogen.

3. Common compounds that turn pink litmus paper to blue are

   _____.

4. When molecules join in a certain way and a new substance is formed,
   a _____ change has taken place.

5. A _____ is formed when two or more
   elements combine.

6. Scientists who study the properties of matter are called _____.

7. The _____ of an object tells how much mass is
   in a particular volume.

8. The smallest part of a substance that is still the substance
   is a _____.

9. Characteristics of matter that help identify it are its _____.

10. The amount of space an object takes up is its _____.

Unit 3 Science Fair Ideas

A science fair project can help you to understand the world around you. Choose a topic that interests you. Then use the scientific method to develop your project. Here's an example:

1. **Problem:** What happens to a steel-wool pad when it is left outside in the rain?

2. **Hypothesis:** The steel-wool pad will rust.

3. **Experimentation:** Materials: 2 steel-wool pads, water, 2 trays.
   • Place a steel-wool pad in each tray.
   • Sprinkle water on one steel pad.
   • Place both trays uncovered on a shelf for two weeks.

4. **Observation:** The wet steel-wool pad begins to rust. The other pad has not changed.

5. **Conclusion:** Water makes the steel in a steel-wool pad rust.

6. **Comparison:** The conclusion and the hypothesis agree.

7. **Presentation:** Research to find why the steel-wool pad rusted. Then prepare a presentation or a report to explain your results. Display both trays, showing the rusty pad and the unchanged pad.

8. **Resources:** Tell the books you used to find why the steel-wool rusted. Tell who helped you to get the materials and set up the experiment.

Other Projects Ideas

1. What are the little bubbles in a can of soda? Do research to find out what the bubbles are.

2. What is the easiest way to open a jar lid when it is stuck? Set up and perform an experiment trying different ways to open a jar lid.

3. How could you show that lemonade is a solution? Do research and then experiment to show how to break down lemonade into its separate ingredients.

Physical Science Grade 5
Answer Key

p. 9 1. T 2. F 3. F 4. F 5. T 6. c. 7. a.

p. 10 8. a. 9. b. 10. d. 11. b. 12. d.

p. 11 1. T 2. F 3. T 4. T 5. T 6. b. 7. d.

p. 12 8. a. 9. b. 10. a. 11. c. 12. b. 13. a. 14. a.

p. 13 1. T 2. T 3. F 4. F 5. T 6. b. 7. b.

p. 14 8. a. 9. d. 10. d. 11. d. 12. b. 13. d. 14. c.

p. 19 1. a. 2. b. 3. d. 4. b.

p. 20 1. The balloons would repel each other. 2. The balloons would repel each other. 3. The balloons would attract each other. 4. Each piece of hair is negatively charged, resulting in each piece repelling the others.

p. 22 1. The ruler picked up the paper. 2. The shavings were attracted to the ruler. 3. Since the objects were attracted to each other, it shows the ruler, paper, and shavings had static electricity. 4. The ruler received extra negative charges. 5. Some of the negative charges of the pieces moved away. This left one end positively charged. The pieces were attracted to the ruler because their positive ends were pulled by the extra negative charges on the ruler.

p. 23 1. Lightning will not reach you as easily if you are inside. 2. Gulf clubs are generally made of metal and attract lightning.

p. 24 3. Cars have rubber tires that do not conduct electricity and can protect against lightning. 4. Lightning strikes the highest objects, so if a bolt strikes near you, it is less likely to strike you. 5. Metal wires can be struck by lightning, which can conduct electricity through the phone. 6. Lightning strikes the highest nearby object. 7. They are often the highest things around and attract lightning. 8. Water is a good conductor of electricity and is likely to be struck. 9. Ledges protrude from their surroundings and are therefore likely to be struck.

p. 25 1. a. 2. d. 3. b.

p. 26 The light should turn on.

p. 28 1. aluminum foil, door key, penny 2. paper, rubber band, pencil 3. Answers will vary. 4. Metals make good conductors.

p. 30 1. All the light bulbs were lit. 2. None of the light bulbs was lit. 3. An electric current can flow through only one path in a series circuit. When one light bulb was unscrewed, the electric current could not flow through the circuit. 4. If one light bulb in a series circuit is not in its socket, then the other light bulbs will not light. If all the light bulbs in a series circuit are in their sockets, then the entire circuit will light.

p. 32 1. All the bulbs were lit. 2. All the bulbs were lit. 3. An electric current can flow through as many paths as there are wires. Each object has two wires which keep the current moving. Even if one light bulb is unscrewed, the others remain lit because there are other paths for the current to travel.

4. A parallel circuit has more than one path for charges. A series circuit has only one path.

p. 33 For 2.-4., drawings may vary.

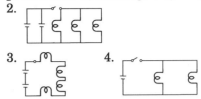

p. 34 1. The balloons would be attracted to each other because of their opposite charges. 2. The person would be negatively charged, so his hair would stand out. 3. Lightning would travel from the cloud to the ground. 4. The bulb will not light because the switch is open. 5. The bulb on the right will light, but the one in the middle will not. 6. The light will not light because the broken fuse causes the circuit to be open.

p. 35 1. Touching the bare wires with the screwdriver caused the circuit to short. 2. The current traveled through the screwdriver. 3. The foil melted. The current got too hot and heated the foil. 4. A fuse can stop the surge of current from damaging the wires and appliances.

p. 36 1. Answers will vary. 2. The current flows through the metal strip and other metal parts of the circuit. 3. The switch is connected to a metal part that is part of the circuit. One end of the metal strip touches the spring near the bottom of the flashlight, and the other end touches the bulb. When you move the switch, you open the circuit. 4. Charges flow from the dry cell to the metal spring, then to the metal strip that is part of the switch. Charges move upward until they reach the metal of the bulb. They enter the bulb, heat the thin wire in the bulb, and move to the metal tip of the bulb. There they enter the terminal of the top of the battery.

p. 38 1. The nails were magnetized when they were rubbed in one direction with the poles of the magnet. 2. The nails lost their magnetism. 3. The nail lost its magnetism. 4. Heating, hammering, or rubbing the nail with a magnet in both directions will destroy magnetism.

p. 39

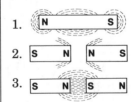

4. *N* stands for *north*; *S* stands for *south*.
5. Answers will vary.

p. 40 1. The space around a magnet is a magnetic field. 2. The poles of a magnet have the strongest magnetic field.

p. 41 1. The paper clip is held by the magnetic field. 2. Nothing happened because paper does not interfere with a magnetic field. 3. The iron nail did, because it is made of a material attracted by a magnet. 4. There was no difference because the poles react the same to metal and nonmetal objects.

p. 42 1. c, a, b, d 2. Check students' work.

p. 44 1. There was a clicking noise. 2. The large-headed nail with the wire wrapped around it is the electromagnet. 3. The circuit is closed when the metal strip touches the small-headed nail. 4. When the circuit is closed, the electric current flows through the wire to make the wire-wrapped nail an electromagnet. The magnetic force pulls the other metal strip to hit the top of the nail to produce a sound.

p. 46 1. It would not be much use because it could not release the iron. 2. When the doorbell is pushed, the electric current is turned on, creating an electromagnet. The iron then moves toward the electromagnet and causes a bell to ring. 3. If the magnet were not an electromagnet, you would not be able to shut off the bell. 4. Turning the key connects the circuit and causes a flow of electricity that turns on the electromagnet.

p. 48 1. The compass needle moved when the magnet moved. 2. The compass needle did not move. 3. The bar magnet was producing an electric current when it was moved through the coil of wire. The compass measured the magnetism produced by the current. 4. The compass acts as a galvanometer. 5. Check students' work.

p. 49 1. Yes; The northern hemisphere is closer to the north magnetic pole. 2. No; The Moon has almost no magnetic field.

p. 50 For 1.-2., answers will vary.

p. 51 For 1.-10., answers will vary.

p. 52 For 1.-10., answers will vary.

p. 54 1. The clouds may produce lightning. It is unsafe to swim during an electrical storm because water is a good conductor. 2. Your fingers could touch the metal prongs, producing a shock. 3. Water is in these rooms, and water conducts electricity. The appliances could come into contact with the water, causing a shock. 4. In an electrical storm, lightning could strike the tree.

p. 60 1. frame of reference 2. motion 3. Answers should reflect an understanding of a frame of reference as a comparison between two objects—one moving and one not moving.

p. 61 1. The walls and other objects in the room appear to move. 2. The pencil is the frame of reference. 3. The pencil appears to move. 4. The walls and other object are the frame of reference.

p. 62 1. 225 mi/50 mph = 4.5 h; about 200 mi/50 mph = 4 h;
75 mi/50 mph = 1.5 h 2. about 275 mi/5 h = 55 mph; 150 mi/2.75 h = 55 mph; about 200 mi/4.5 h = 45 mph

p. 64 1. Answers will vary. 2. Answers will vary. 3. Since the speed for any one trial may be atypical, finding the average speed for several trials lessens the possibility of an inaccurate measurement. 4. Answers will vary. Possible responses: amount of time it took the marble to reach the tape; friction.

p. 66 1. 64–48 = 16 km/hr (10 mi/hr) east 2. The difference in velocity tells how fast the faster vehicle is pulling away from the slower one. 3. Relative velocities could be used to calculate how much sooner one vehicle would arrive at a certain location or how long it would take one vehicle to overtake the other. 4. 56 + 40 = 96 km/hr (60 mi/hr) 5. 1,012 km/hr (629 mi/hr) east

p. 67 A. Step 2: The paper towel moves, but the cup should not move. B. Step 3: The cup should move, but the paper clip should remain in the same position—on top of the pencil mark. A pull on the cup caused it to move. No force was exerted on the paper clip, so it stayed at rest.

p. 68 1. B 2. C 3. A 4. A 5. B 6. C

p. 70 1. Answers will vary. 2. Answers will vary, but the number of vibrations should be less for the rock than the washer. 3. It was easier to move the washer. Since the washer had less mass, less force was needed to move it. 4. The rock had greater inertia since it had more mass. 5. The rock had greater mass, because it was made up of more matter.

p. 71 1. Moving the bottle forward made the bubble move forward. Moving it backwards made the bubble move backwards. A left turn made the bubble move left, too. 2. Velocity changes when direction changes. Acceleration is the rate of change in velocity.

p. 72 1. a. ball hitting bat; b. positive 2. a. friction on brakes; b. negative 3. a. push of rocket; b. positive 4. a. dog pulling; b. negative

p. 74 1. pennies 2. Answers will vary. The distance between each drop of water and the next is a measure of acceleration and should have increased as the truck progressed. 3. Answers will vary. Distance was greater between those water drops falling from the truck without sand than between those falling from the truck carrying sand. 4. The truck without the sand accelerated faster, because the distance between the drops of water was greater. 5. When the sand was removed, the truck's mass was decreased and its acceleration increased.

p. 75 1. A 2. C 3. B 4. D 5. B 6. D 7. A, C

p. 76 1. c. 2. d. 3. a. 4. b. 5. Possible answer: When hanging from the ceiling, the piñata and its contents have gravitational potential energy. As the children hit the piñata with a stick, they are using mechanical energy. When the piñata breaks, the candy and toys falling out have kinetic energy.

p. 78 1. The greatest potential energy is when the rubber band is tightly wound before it is about to spin back in the other direction. 2. The twisted rubber band provides potential energy. 3. It is converted when the rubber band unwinds and the carousel spins. 4. The release of the rubber band's potential energy caused the momentum of the carousel, allowing it to rotate after the energy of the rubber band stopped.

p. 80 1. The nickel caused the pennies to move farther 2. The nickel had the greater momentum because it had more mass.

p. 81 1. a. Arrows face in and begin at each wrestlers' shoulders. b. Arrows face out and begin at the first person in line. 2. a. push b. push or pull c. push or pull d. pull e. push or pull f. pull g. push h. pull

p. 82 1. He is using the rings, and he is doing work by pulling himself up. 2. He is using muscles in his arms and upper body. 3. He pulls down on the rings to pull himself up. 4. The leg muscles help to kick the ball. The force of the kick is in a forward direction.

p. 84 1. It moved backward, in a direction away from the carton. 2. It moved forward, in the opposite direction of the air. 3. The air coming out of the balloon was the action force. 4. The forward movement of the carton was the reaction force. 5. Newton's third law states that for every action, there is an equal and opposite reaction. 6. A propeller pushes backward against the water, like the air flowing from the balloon. The water pushes forward just as it did in the experiment.

p. 85 1. action: book pushes down-arrow points down from book to table; reaction: table pushes up-arrow points up from table to book 2. action: cloth of parachute pushes down-arrow points down from cloth to ground; reaction: air pushes up-arrow points from ground to parachute 3. action: child kicks ball forward-arrow points from foot to ball; reaction: ball pushes back on foot-arrow points from ball to foot 4. action: engine pushes gas out-arrow points from mid-rocket down to boosters; reaction: engine moves forward-arrow points up from mid-rocket to tip of rocket

p. 86 1. reference point 2. distance 3. time 4. velocity 5. speed 6. force 7. mass 8. inertia 9. inertia 10. force 11. accelerated

p. 88 1. They hit the ground at the same time. 2. The force of gravity varies according to mass. The force of gravity increases as the mass increases so that it makes them fall at the same time. 3. A force is a push or pull. Gravity is a pull that draws all objects toward the center of the Earth.

p. 89 1. Earth; The largest force is required to lift the objects on Earth. 2. Planet Y; The least amount of force is required on planet Y.

p. 90 3. Earth's gravity = 5 x planet Y's gravity 4. Earth's gravity = 2.5 x planet X's gravity 5. planet X's gravity = 2 x planet Y's gravity 6. Object 5 requires the greatest force to lift it. 7. 5, 1, 3, 2, 4 8. Object 1 has 4 times the mass of object 4.

p. 92 1. the washer 2. Divide the total time for ten cycles by 10. 3. The longer pendulum has a longer period.

p. 93 1. gravity 2. collision of 2 objects 3. The string keeps the ball in circular motion until it is cut, then the ball travels in a straight path.

p. 94 1. The forces were the force caused by squeezing the bottle, which made the cup move up, and gravity, which pulled it downward. 2. The downward force of gravity was not as strong as the upward force of the plug. 3. No; balanced forces do not cause movement.

p. 95 1. fluid 2. sliding 3. sliding 4. fluid 5. rolling 6. sliding

p. 96 1. The oil decreased the amount of time it took the eraser to slide down the ramp. 2. The fluid friction created less force than the sliding friction. 3. Oil reduces friction between the surfaces of moving parts in machines so they run more smoothly and longer.

p. 97 1. Answers will vary. 2. Answers will vary. 3. Newton's first law of motion states that objects that are moving in one direction tend to keep moving in that direction unless an outside force acts on them. In this case, if someone slams on the brakes, even though the car slows and stops, the bodies in the car will keep moving forward. Lighter objects, such as children, are thrown farther than heavier objects. Seatbelts stop this forward movement, so they are important. Otherwise, objects would hit the windshield, or dashboard, or be thrown out of the car.

p. 103 1. Matter takes up space and has volume. 2. Possible answers: color, taste, odor, and boiling point. 3. Possible responses: It has a round shape, with a bumpy texture. It has an orange color. It is sweet to taste. It is juicy on the inside.

p. 104 1. Standard units are always the same. If standard units are used, anyone can make the same measurements and get the same results. 2. Length: meter, m; Mass: gram, g; Volume of solids: cubic centimeter, cm^3; Temperature: degrees Celsius, °C

p. 105 1. 92.4 2. 1.8 3. 134.2 4. 63.8

p. 106 1. 120 cm 2. 784 g 3. 5.4 m 4. 67.2 km 5. 5.7 L

p. 107 1. a. gas b. solid c. liquid 2. Water drops form on a glass containing a cold drink because the water vapor (gas) in the air is cooled when it touches the cold glass. It causes the water to change to its liquid phase. 3. Water is in its liquid state and changes to water vapor when heat is added.

p. 108 1. gas 2. liquid 3. solid 4. gas 5. solid 6. Molecules in a liquid slide over each other and move faster than molecules in a solid, which are packed tightly and only vibrate.

p. 110 1. Solid; It had a definite shape. 2. Liquid; Liquids take the shape of their container. 3. An increase in temperature caused the cube to melt. 4. The level of water decreased. 5. Water from the container evaporated into the air. 6. If ice melted in fruit juice, the taste of the juice would be weakened.

p. 111 1. If the balance is weighted in one direction, the measurement of mass will not be accurate. 2. Find the sum of the gram measures. 3. Answers will vary.

p. 112 1. Ruler; The sides of the tank are straight. 2. Water in a measuring cup; The keys have an irregular shape that cannot be measured with a ruler. 3. Answers will vary.

Physical Science 5, SV 3764-X